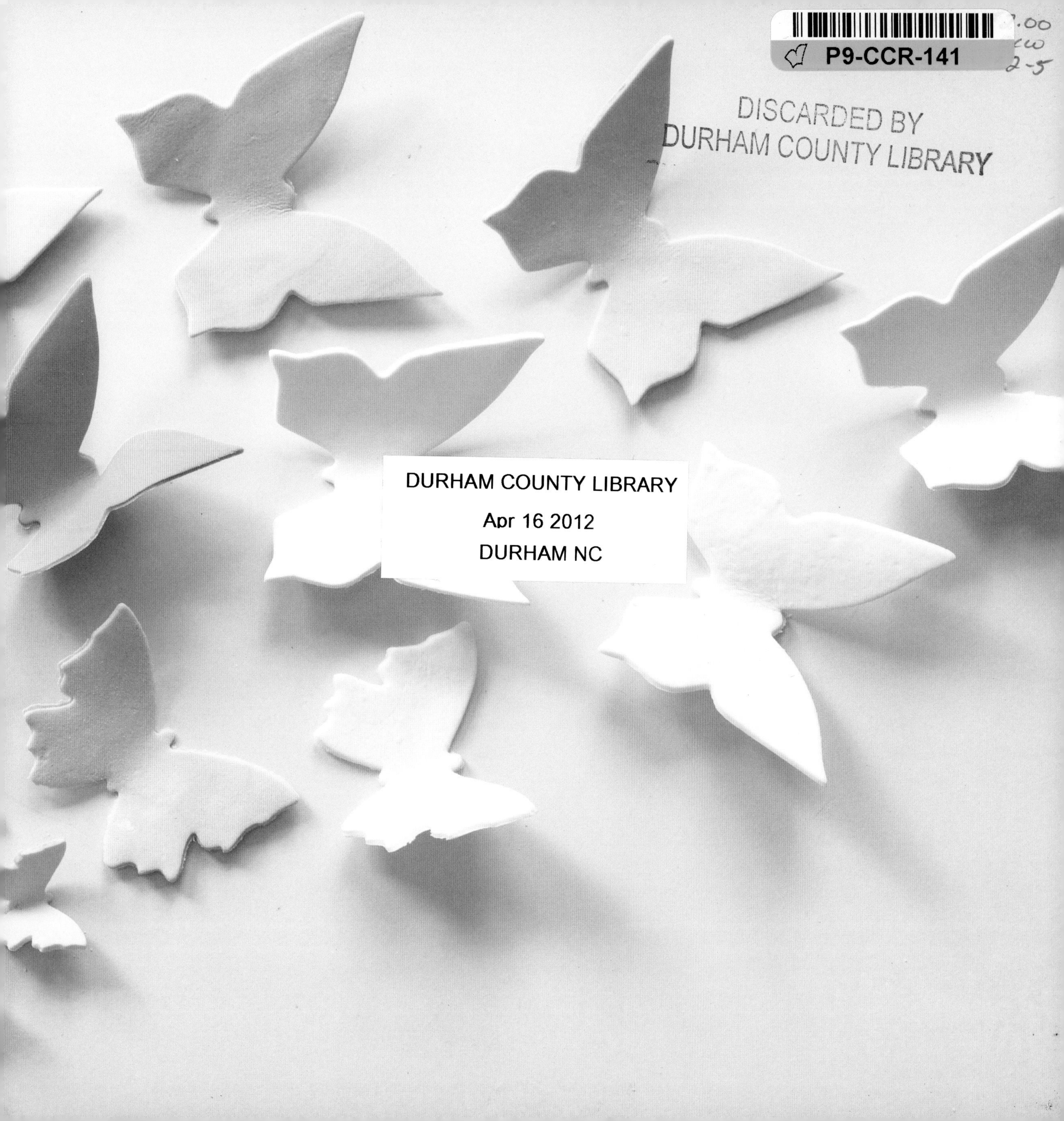

Make, bake & celebrate!

Make, bake & celebrate!

How to create beautifully decorated cakes for every occasion

Annie Rigg

photography by
Kate Whitaker

RYLAND
PETERS
& SMALL
LONDON NEW YORK

Senior Designer Iona Hoyle
Commissioning Editor Céline Hughes
Production Gordana Simakovic
Art Director Leslie Harrington
Editorial Director Julia Charles

Prop Stylist Liz Belton
Indexer Hilary Bird

First published in 2012
by Ryland Peters & Small
20–21 Jockey's Fields
London WC1R 4BW
and
519 Broadway, 5th Floor
New York, NY 10012

www.rylandpeters.com

Text © Annie Rigg 2012
Design and photographs
© Ryland Peters & Small 2012

Printed in China

10 9 8 7 6 5 4 3 2 1

ISBN: 978-1-84975-221-3

A CIP record for this book is available
from the British Library.
CIP data has been applied for from the
Library of Congress.

notes

• All spoon measurements are level,
unless otherwise specified.

• Ovens should be preheated to the
specified temperature. Recipes in this
book were tested using a regular oven.
If using a fan-assisted/convection oven,
follow the manufacturer's instructions
for adjusting temperatures.

• Recipes containing raw or partially
cooked egg, or raw fish or shellfish,
should not be served to the very young,
very old, anyone with a compromised
immune system or pregnant women.

• All butter is unsalted, unless otherwise
specified.

contents

sprinkles & sparkles

When I think of parties or celebrations, I think of friends, family, good times – and of course, cakes, which in truth, feature top of the list. Any excuse – birthdays, weddings, Halloween and Christmas – and my mind starts racing with thoughts of layer cakes, cupcakes, tantalizing flavours, luscious frostings and myriad decorations.

In this book you'll find a collection of recipes that are far from the everyday run-of-the-mill cakes; these are crowd pleasers and cakes with wow factor, cakes that require a special occasion, a party, a celebration! This kind of cake demands that you bring out your best table linen and fancy chinaware to set the table with. These cakes, being something special, shout "look at me!" and really should be placed centre stage in the middle of the table, served on cake stands and eaten with delicate silver cake forks.

Some of the simpler cakes in this book need nothing more than a crown of candles, while others need a couple of days' advance planning and preparation. All of the more elaborate cakes can and should be, in part, prepared in advance.

Most of the recipes are large enough to feed a crowd: a triple-layer cake will happily feed 10 people, and a triple-tier rich chocolate wedding cake will feed around 60 guests.

It's probably not every day that you make cakes for special occasions, so set aside plenty of time to plan and bake your creations – they are definitely not to be rushed and knocked out in an afternoon. Some triple-tier cakes can be baked over a couple of days, so plan backwards from the day you plan to serve it. For example, you can make any gum-paste decorations up to a week before you finally decorate the cake; this gives them plenty of time to dry. The brandied cherries in The Ultimate Black Forest Cake can be made a few days before the cake – in fact their flavour will improve over time.

There are a few simple rules to follow with cake baking, and as most of these cakes can take time, it will help to take note.

I always use good-quality cake pans. It really does pay to spend a little extra for better quality – they'll last longer, bake evenly and won't misshape or buckle in the oven.

If you're making multi-layered cakes, I would recommend that you make sure all the baking pans you use are the same brand and exactly the same size. This way the layers will stack up perfectly.

As always with baking, you really must use the best and freshest ingredients that you can afford: free-range, happy eggs, pure vanilla extract, unsalted butter and good, pure chocolate. Dried fruit and nuts should be fresh – old nuts can give your cakes a rancid and bitter taste. Wash and dry citrus fruit before grating the zest and always use fresh, firm fruit. If you don't, it will be hard to grate, and the zest and juice will lack punch.

I always keep an oven thermometer in my oven. It's very difficult to be accurate without one, and it helps to determine where your oven is the hottest.

So, from now on, you have no excuse to let an event or celebration pass without cake. Take your best frilliest apron, get creative with the frosting and pull out all the stops with the piping bag. In my mind, a party is not a party without cake!

the basics

basic cake recipes

For the best results when embarking on any baking, there are a few golden rules that you'd be wise to follow.

Make sure that you weigh and measure the ingredients accurately. Use measuring spoons where necessary as regular cutlery can vary enormously in size – the teaspoon that I use to stir my tea is not necessarily the same size as yours.

Prepare your cake pans according to the recipe before you even start to mix the cake ingredients. I use unsalted butter and nonstick baking parchment to grease and line my pans and sometimes a light dusting of flour if necessary.

If you are using moulded or kugelhopf pans, which are harder to grease, I suggest that you pop the empty pans into the fridge for 15 minutes before brushing the insides with melted butter and dusting with flour. This will help you to be certain that every corner and fold has been thoroughly greased.

When making traditional fruit cakes, I recommend that you wrap the outside of the cake pan in a collar of a double thickness of either brown paper or baking parchment and tie it securely with kitchen twine. This will prevent the outside of the cake browning too quickly during the longer cooking time.

Preheat the oven to the correct temperature using an oven thermometer if possible. This will give you greater accuracy and is all the more important if your oven is on the temperamental side. Position the oven shelves at the correct height in the oven for your pans.

Have all your ingredients ready at room temperature – this generally applies to any dairy produce such as butter, buttermilk, sour cream, milk and eggs.

I find it easier to make my cakes using a stand mixer. It not only makes light work of creaming butter and sugar together, it also whips up beautiful meringues, and in a fraction of the time than it would take by hand. Failing that, you can also use an electric hand whisk.

Rubber spatulas are also an essential part of a cake baker's kit, making it easy to scrape down bowls and to ensure that every last spoonful of cake mixture makes it into the cake pans, and not onto the fingers and into the mouths of any willing helpers/washer-uppers you may have around.

If you are making multiple cake layers from one batch of mixture, I would suggest that you weigh the batter evenly into the prepared pans to ensure that each cake layer will be the exact same depth once baked.

When you are planning to stack layers of cake or make a cake that should be completely flat on top, if the baked cake has risen, you will need to level it off using a long serrated knife to create a perfectly flat surface.

basic vanilla cake

350 g/2⅔ cups plain/all-purpose flour

3 teaspoons baking powder

1 teaspoon bicarbonate of/baking soda

a pinch of salt

225 g/2 sticks butter, soft

350 g/1¾ cups (caster) sugar

4 large eggs

1 teaspoon vanilla extract

250 ml/1 cup buttermilk, room temperature

two 23-cm/9-inch or three 20-cm/8-inch round cake pans, greased and baselined with greased baking parchment

Preheat the oven to 180°C (350°F) Gas 4.

Sift together the flour, baking powder, bicarbonate of/baking soda and salt.

Cream the butter and sugar in the bowl of a stand mixer until really pale and light – at least 3–4 minutes.

Lightly beat the eggs and vanilla together. Gradually add to the creamed butter in 4 or 5 additions, mixing well between each addition and scraping down the bowl from time to time with a rubber spatula.

Add the sifted dry ingredients to the bowl alternately with the buttermilk. Mix until smooth.

Now turn to the relevant recipe and continue with the instructions, or if you want to bake the cake, divide the mixture evenly between the prepared pans and spread level with a palette knife. Bake the cakes on the middle shelf of the preheated oven for about 25 minutes or until a skewer inserted into the middle comes out clean.

Let cool in the pans for 3–4 minutes, then turn out onto a wire rack to cool completely.

basic chocolate cake

125 g/4 oz. dark/bittersweet chocolate, chopped

300 g/2⅓ cups plain/all-purpose flour

25 g/3 tablespoons cocoa powder

2 teaspoons bicarbonate of/baking soda

½ teaspoon baking powder

a pinch of salt

125 g/1 stick butter, soft

200 g/1 cup (caster) sugar

200 g/1 cup packed light brown soft sugar

4 large eggs, beaten

2 teaspoons vanilla extract

225 ml/1 cup sour cream, room temperature

175 ml/¾ cup boiling water

two 23-cm/9-inch or three 20-cm/8-inch round cake pans, greased and baselined with greased baking parchment

Preheat the oven to 180°C (350°F) Gas 4.

Melt the chocolate in a heatproof bowl set over a pan of barely simmering water, stir until smooth, then let cool slightly.

Sift together the flour, cocoa powder, bicarbonate of/baking soda, baking powder and salt.

Cream the butter and both sugars in the bowl of a stand mixer for 3–4 minutes.

Gradually add the beaten eggs to the creamed butter in 4 or 5 additions, mixing well between each addition and scraping down the bowl from time to time with a rubber spatula. Add the vanilla and melted chocolate and mix again until combined.

Mix one-third of the sifted dry ingredients into the mixture, then half the sour cream. Repeat this process and finish with the last third of dry ingredients. Mix until smooth. Slowly pour in the boiling water and mix until smooth.

Now turn to the relevant recipe and continue with the instructions, or if you want to bake the cake, divide the mixture evenly between the prepared pans and spread level with a palette knife. Bake the cakes on the middle shelf of the preheated oven for about 25 minutes or until a skewer inserted into the middle comes out clean.

Let cool in the pans for 3–4 minutes, then turn out onto a wire rack to cool completely.

whisked almond cake

50 g/3 tablespoons butter

50 g/½ cup ground almonds

150 g/1 cup plus 3 tablespoons plain/
all-purpose flour

1 teaspoon baking powder

a pinch of salt

6 large eggs

150 g/¾ cup (caster) sugar

1 teaspoon vanilla extract

*two 23-cm/9-inch or three 20-cm/8-inch round
cake pans, greased and baselined with greased
baking parchment*

Preheat the oven to 180°C (350°F) Gas 4.

Melt the butter and let cool slightly.

Sift together the ground almonds, flour, baking
powder and salt.

Put the eggs, sugar and vanilla in the bowl of a
stand mixer and whisk on medium–high speed
until the mixture has trebled in volume, is thick,
pale, very light and will leave a ribbon trail
when the whisk is lifted from the bowl.

Using a large metal spoon, gently fold
the sifted dry ingredients into the egg
mixture. Pour the melted butter
around the inside edge of the bowl
and gently fold in.

Now turn to the relevant recipe and
continue with the instructions, or if you
want to bake the cake, divide the mixture evenly
between the prepared cake pans, spread level
and bake on the middle shelf of the preheated
oven for about 20 minutes or until golden,
well risen and a skewer inserted in the middle
comes out clean.

Let cool in the cake pans for a couple of
minutes before turning out onto a wire rack
to cool completely.

light fruit cake

100 g/⅔ cup undyed glacé cherries

50 g/⅓ cup blanched almonds

50 g/⅓ cup mixed candied peel

75 g/½ cup dried cranberries (optional)

500 g/1 lb. mixed dried fruit (sultanas,
[golden] raisins and currants)

grated zest of 1 lemon

grated zest of 1 orange

275 g/2¼ cups strong white bread flour or
plain/all-purpose flour

50 g/½ cup ground almonds

1 teaspoon baking powder

a pinch of salt

225 g/15 tablespoons butter, soft

150 g/¾ cup golden caster/raw cane sugar

75 g/⅓ cup golden syrup/light corn syrup

3 large eggs, lightly beaten

2 tablespoons brandy or milk

*deep, 20-cm/8-inch round cake pan, lined with
a double layer of greased baking parchment*

extra baking parchment

kitchen twine

Preheat the oven to 150°C (300°F) Gas 2.

Wrap the outside of the cake pan in a double thickness of baking parchment and secure with kitchen twine.

Rinse the glacé cherries under warm water, thoroughly pat dry on kitchen paper/paper towels, cut in half and tip into a large bowl. Roughly chop the almonds and add to the bowl along with the mixed candied peel, dried cranberries, mixed dried fruit and the grated lemon and orange zest. Mix well and set aside.

Sift together the flour, ground almonds, baking powder, and salt.

Cream the butter, sugar and syrup in the bowl of a stand mixer until really pale and light – at least 3–4 minutes.

Gradually add the beaten eggs to the creamed butter in 4 or 5 additions, mixing well between each addition and scraping down the bowl from time to time with a rubber spatula.

Add the sifted dry ingredients to the bowl using a large metal spoon. Add the dried fruit mixture and the brandy, stir to thoroughly combine and spoon into the prepared cake pan, scraping the mixture from the bowl using a rubber spatula. Spread level and bake just below the middle of the preheated oven for 1 hour 40 minutes or until a skewer inserted in the middle of the cake comes out clean. If the top of the cake is browning too quickly, loosely cover with a sheet of baking parchment.

Let cool completely in the cake pan on a wire rack. When cold, wrap in clingfilm/plastic wrap until ready to decorate.

classic rich fruit cake

150 g/1 cup undyed glacé cherries
200 g/1⅓ cups raisins
200 g/1⅓ cups currants
200 g/1⅓ cups sultanas/golden raisins
100 g/⅔ cup mixed candied peel, finely chopped
100 g/⅔ cup roughly chopped almonds
2 teaspoons mixed spice/apple pie spice
2 teaspoons vanilla extract
grated zest and juice of 1 lemon
grated zest and juice of 1 orange
200 ml/¾ cup brandy, marsala or whisky
200 g/1⅔ cups plain/all-purpose flour
50 g/½ cup gound almonds
1 teaspoon baking powder
a pinch of salt
250 g/2 sticks butter, soft
200 g/1 cup light muscovado sugar
50 g/3 tablespoons golden syrup/light corn syrup
4 large eggs, beaten

deep, 23-cm/9-inch round cake pan, lined with a double layer of greased baking parchment
baking parchment
kitchen twine

Wrap the outside of the cake pan in a double thickness of baking parchment and secure with kitchen twine.

Rinse the glacé cherries under warm water, thoroughly pat dry on kitchen paper/paper towels, cut in half and tip into a large saucepan.

Add the dried fruit, almonds, spice, vanilla, grated orange and lemon zests and the juice and brandy to the saucepan. Set over low–medium heat and warm until the liquid is just below boiling. Immediately remove from the heat, stir and leave until cold and the fruit has become plump, juicy and has absorbed almost all the liquid about 3–4 hours. Stir the mixture every 3 minutes or so while cools.

Preheat the oven to 150°C (300°F) Gas 2.

Sift together the flour, ground almonds, baking powder and salt.

Cream the butter, sugar and syrup in the bowl of a stand mixer until really pale and light – at least 3–4 minutes.

Gradually add the beaten eggs to the creamed butter in 4 or 5 additions, mixing well between each addition and scraping down the bowl from time to time with a rubber spatula.

Add the sifted dry ingredients to the bowl using a large metal spoon. Add the dried fruit mixture and any remaining liquid, stir to thoroughly combine and spoon into the prepared cake pan, scraping the mixture from the bowl using a rubber spatula. Spread level and bake just below the middle of the preheated oven for about 2 hours or until a skewer inserted in the middle of the cake comes out clean. If the top of the cake is browning too quickly, loosely cover with a sheet of baking parchment.

Let cool completely in the cake pan on a wire rack. When cold, wrap in clingfilm/plastic wrap until ready to decorate.

basic frostings & fillings

No self-respecting celebration cake is complete without its finger-licking frosting and filling. And for some eager cake-eaters that I know, the frosting is the best part and they will happily scoop up spoonfuls without needing even a crumb of cake! I'm mentioning no names... Most of these frostings can be piped into elaborate swirls and rosettes or simply spread in generous swooshes using a palette knife. Or eaten straight from the bowl if your name is Kate.

Once the cake is baked and you've made the frosting, it's a good time to get the kids involved. Only attempt this if you are happy for your cake to look a little less refined and a little more lovingly homemade! If it's a surprise for Father's Day or a a birthday, for example, kids will love to help out and get messy with a piping bag. Start with something very simple, like the Lemon Poppy Seed Cake on page 28, or let them roll the Mini Iced Gem Cakes in the sugar strands/jimmies on page 62. Older or more confident children might like to try piping the rosettes around the Chocolate Dazzle Drop Cake on page 50. However, do be wary of letting children lick the spoon if the frosting contains raw eggs.

chocolate ganache

This rich chocolate frosting is an ideal partner for a more sophisticated cake. Give it the quality it deserves by using chocolate with 70% cocoa solids.

200 g/6½ oz.dark/bittersweet chocolate, finely chopped
225 ml/1 cup double/heavy cream
2 tablespoons light brown soft sugar
50 g/3 tablespoons butter, diced

Put the chocolate in a medium bowl.

Put the cream and sugar in a small saucepan and heat until only just boiling and the sugar has dissolved. Pour the hot cream over the chocolate and let melt for 5 minutes. Add the butter and stir gently until smooth. Let thicken to the desired consistency before using.

cream cheese frosting

Always use good-quality cream cheese for frosting, as some brands are more salty than others, and add the honey or maple syrup according to taste.

300 g/10 oz. cream cheese
50 g/3 tablespoons butter, soft
2–3 tablespoons (clear) honey or maple syrup
1 teaspoon vanilla extract or the seeds from ½ vanilla pod/bean

Tip the cream cheese into a bowl, add the butter and mix until smooth. Gradually add the honey or maple syrup to taste. Add the vanilla and mix until smooth.

chocolate fudge frosting

I like to use this frosting for kids' cakes as it is a less intense chocolate hit, but it's by no means any less delicious. It can be used as a filling and frosting for either chocolate or vanilla cakes – just don't forget to pile on the chocolate shavings or sugar sprinkles.

350 g/12 oz. dark/semisweet chocolate, chopped
225 g/15 tablespoons butter, diced
175 ml/⅔ cup milk
1 teaspoon vanilla extract
350 g/3 cups icing/confectioners' sugar, sifted

Melt the chocolate and butter in a heatproof bowl set over a pan of barely simmering water. Do not let the base of the bowl touch the water. Stir until smooth and thoroughly combined. Remove from the heat and cool slightly.

In another bowl whisk together the milk, vanilla and sugar until smooth. Add the melted chocolate and butter and stir until smooth. Let thicken to the desired consistency before using.

chocolate cream frosting

This is a silky, luscious affair and is ideal for use on smaller, delicate cakes.

100 g/½ cup (caster) sugar
½ teaspoon instant coffee granules or coffee extract
4 large egg yolks
1 teaspoon vanilla extract
200 g/6½ oz. dark/bittersweet chocolate, chopped
300 g/2½ sticks butter, soft

Tip the sugar into a small pan with 6 tablespoons water. Bring to the boil to dissolve the sugar, then boil steadily for 2–3 minutes until slightly thickened. Dissolve the coffee granules in 1 teaspoon boiling water and add to the syrup. Alternatively, add the coffee extract straight to the sugar syrup.

Place the egg yolks and vanilla in the bowl of a stand mixer and whisk to combine. Whisking constantly, pour the hot syrup into the yolks in a steady stream. Continue whisking on high speed until the mixture is thick, cold and will hold a ribbon trail when the whisk is lifted from the mixture.

Melt the chocolate in a heatproof bowl set over a pan of barely simmering water. Do not let the base of the bowl touch the water. Let cool slightly.

Gradually add the butter to the egg mixture, beating well between each addition. Add the cooled chocolate and stir to thoroughly combine.

royal icing

You can make royal icing using raw egg whites, but if you prefer not to, royal icing sugar/mix is available from supermarkets and sugarcraft stores.

1 large egg white
250–300 g/1¾–2⅓ cups icing/confectioners' sugar, sifted

Using a balloon whisk, beat the egg white until foamy. Gradually add the icing/confectioners' sugar and whisk until the desired stiffness is reached – for piping, the icing should hold a solid ribbon trail when the whisk is lifted from the bowl. Cover with clingfilm/plastic wrap until ready to use.

An easier method of making royal icing is to use royal icing sugar/mix. This is perfect if you prefer not to use raw egg whites, too. It contains dried powdered egg white and simply needs sifting into a bowl and beating or whisking with cold water until the desired consistency is achieved.

marshmallow frosting

The perfect frosting for a delicately flavoured base, this encases a cake in a cloud of soft meringue without overpowering and taking over. You must use this as soon as it's made, as it will set as it cools, making spreading impossible.

250 g/1¼ cups caster/superfine sugar
4 large egg whites
a pinch of salt
sugar thermometer

Put all the ingredients with 1 tablespoon water in a medium heatproof bowl set over a pan of simmering water. Whisk slowly with a balloon whisk until the sugar has dissolved and the mixture is foamy. Continue to cook and whisk until the mixture reaches 60°C/140°F on a sugar thermometer – about 4 minutes.

Quickly pour the mixture into the bowl of a stand mixer and whisk on medium–high speed for 3 minutes, or until thick and glossy. Use immediately.

meringue buttercream

This is my all-time favourite frosting. For a buttercream it's surprisingly light due to the addition of meringue. It's enormously versatile and can be flavoured with vanilla, lemon or coffee extract, or even strawberry jam and lemon curd. It's important to add the butter only once the meringue is cooled otherwise it will melt and make the frosting curdle.

275 g/1⅓ cups caster/superfine sugar
4 large egg whites
a pinch of salt
350 g/3 sticks butter, soft and diced
1 teaspoon vanilla extract or the seeds from ½ vanilla pod/bean
sugar thermometer

Put the sugar, egg whites and salt in a medium heatproof bowl set over a pan of simmering water. Whisk slowly with a balloon whisk until the sugar has completely dissolved and the mixture is foamy. Continue to cook and whisk until the mixture reaches 60°C/140°F on a sugar thermometer – about 4 minutes.

Quickly pour the mixture into the bowl of a stand mixer and whisk on medium–high speed for 3 minutes, or until cooled, thick, stiff and glossy. Gradually add the butter, beating constantly, until the frosting is smooth. Fold in the vanilla and use immediately.

chocolate meringue buttercream

This is a slightly lighter alternative to Chocolate Fudge or Chocolate Cream Frosting and is perfect for piping. If you have any left over, it can be stored in the fridge for a couple of days. Bring back to room temperature and beat until smooth before using to top a batch of cupcakes or whatever takes your fancy. I would use chocolate with 70% cocoa solids for this frosting.

300 g/10 oz. dark/bittersweet chocolate, chopped
225 g/1 cup plus 2 tablespoons caster/superfine sugar
4 large egg whites
a pinch of salt
350 g/3 sticks butter, soft and chopped
sugar thermometer

Melt the chocolate in a heatproof bowl set over a pan of barely simmering water. Do not let the base of the bowl touch the water.

Put the sugar, egg whites and salt in a medium heatproof bowl set over a pan of simmering water. Whisk slowly with a balloon whisk until the sugar has completely dissolved and the mixture is foamy. Continue to cook and whisk until the mixture reaches 60°C/140°F on a sugar thermometer – about 4 minutes.

Quickly pour the mixture into the bowl of a stand mixer and whisk on medium–high speed for 3 minutes, or until cooled, thick, stiff and glossy. Gradually add the butter, beating constantly, until the frosting is smooth. Fold in the melted chocolate and use immediately.

mocha meringue buttercream

Make the Chocolate Meringue Buttercream as described above. Add 2–3 teaspoons instant coffee granules dissolved in 1 teaspoon boiling water when you add the melted chocolate.

rum or brandy syrup

150 g/¾ cup (caster) sugar
3 tablespoons rum, brandy or Amaretto

Tip the sugar into a small saucepan with 150 ml/⅔ cup water. Bring slowly to the boil over medium heat, stirring to dissolve the sugar. Continue to simmer for 2–3 minutes until slightly thickened. Remove from the heat and add the rum, brandy or Amaretto. Let cool before using. Any leftover syrup will keep well in an airtight container or screw-top jar in the fridge for a couple of weeks.

hazelnut liqueur syrup

50 g/¼ cup (caster) sugar
125 ml/½ cup water
70 ml/5 tablespoons hazelnut liqueur, such as Frangelico

Heat the sugar and water in a small saucepan to dissolve the sugar, then bring to the boil and continue to cook until the syrup has reduced by half. Remove from the heat and add the hazelnut liqueur. Stir and let cool before using.

lemon curd

This is an ideal way of using up leftover egg yolks if you've been making meringues or meringue frosting. But seeing as homemade lemon curd is so utterly delicious anyway, I would suggest making it and then using up the leftover egg whites to make meringues!

6 large egg yolks
grated zest and juice of 3 lemons
175 g/¾ cup plus 2 tablespoons (caster) sugar
75 g/5 tablespoons unsalted butter
a pinch of salt

Combine the egg yolks, lemon juice, sugar and butter in a medium heatproof bowl set over a pan of simmering water. Do not let the base of the bowl touch the water. Whisk the mixture to combine, then stir constantly for about 5–7 minutes until thickened and the curd will coat the back of a wooden spoon.

Remove from the heat and pass through a fine nylon sieve/strainer into a bowl. Add the lemon zest, stir until smooth and cover the surface of the curd with clingfilm/plastic wrap to prevent a skin from forming. Let cool completely, then refrigerate until firm before using.

decorating techniques

piping bags

If you are new to piping, I would recommend that you practise piping on some baking parchment first to get a feel for how the frosting behaves.

Piping nozzles/tips and bags come in a variety of sizes and shapes. With a small selection of nozzles/tips you can create myriad patterns. As for the piping bags, I would suggest that you have one or two larger, plastic-coated piping bags (rather than woven or cloth), which are ideal for piping meringues. You should also have a stash of plastic disposable piping bags for smaller decorative projects. These come in multipacks and are invaluable for fine patterns, dots, writing, outlines, etc. You simply fill them with the frosting, snip off the end to a fine point and get piping!

I find special nozzles for making leaf shapes and star-shaped nozzles/tips in assorted sizes are fantastically useful and can be used in a variety of ways to create simple yet pretty results.

ready to roll icing

Ready-to-roll royal and fondant icing can be found in most supermarkets. It comes in blocks of varying sizes and is widely available in white or ivory, as well as many colours from specialist sugarcraft suppliers (see page 128). However, it is easy to tint using food colouring pastes. Fondant icing sets slightly softer than royal icing, but they are interchangeable in most recipes.

When covering a cake with royal or fondant icing, you ideally want a silky-smooth surface without lumps, bumps or creases (although these can usually be hidden with strategically placed ribbons, flowers and piping).

Carefully roll the icing out to an even thickness on a work surface that's dusted with icing/confectioners' sugar. The icing needs to be large enough to cover the top and sides of the cake in one piece. Roll the icing around and over the rolling pin and unroll it over the cake from the back of the cake to the front (or left to right) ensuring that it is centred and that there is an equal amount of icing covering all sides. Dust your (clean) hands with more sugar and use the palm of your hands to gently smooth the icing into place, getting rid of any creases as you go. Use a small, sharp knife to trim off any excess icing from the bottom of the cake.

embossing

Use embossing tools to create eye-catching patterns on either gum or sugar paste, fondant or royal icing. They are available from cake decorating stores or online and usually come in geometric shapes, fancy patterns, flowers and leaf shapes. Alternatively, look around your kitchen and you'll find embossers in unlikely places: the fine side of a grater, the underside of antique silver cutlery and the points of piping nozzles/tips.

using dowel rods & stacking tiered cakes

For cakes that require extra support when being stacked, you'll need to use dowelling, which is available from cake decorating and sugarcraft suppliers. Dowel rods are plastic supports about the thickness of a pencil which can be cut to size using small shears. This acts as a set of pillars inside the finished cake onto which the next cake (on a cake board) will sit without sinking into the cake below. See page 100 for step-by-step pictures and instructions on stacking tiered cakes using dowel rods.

crystallizing flowers & fruit

This is an incredibly simple yet stunning way to decorate cakes and requires no specialist kit or artistic genius.

If you are using fresh flower petals, make sure they are cut from fresh, non-toxic, unsprayed and untreated flowers, and better still, cut from your own garden.

Rose petals, small rose buds, pansies, violets, primroses and nasturtiums all make beautiful crystallized petals. See page 78 for imstructions on crystallizing roses, for example.

Fresh berries and fruit are also perfect for crystallizing. Try grapes, red and white currants, cherries, cranberries, physallis/cape gooseberries and even small apples and pears. The cake on page 112 is a lovely example of how best to showcase crystallized fruits.

Once made, petals and fruits will dry and harden in about 2–4 hours and they are best used within 48 hours of making, as their colour will start to fade.

chocolate shavings

Showering a cake with chocolate shavings is a simple yet stunning way of decorating a cake (it also hides a multitude of icing sins!).

Break 250 g/9 oz. milk, dark/bittersweet or white chocolate into pieces, tip into a heatproof bowl and set over a pan of barely simmering water. Do not let the bottom of the bowl touch the water. Melt the chocolate and stir until smooth. Pour the chocolate onto the underside of a baking sheet and spread to a depth of around 5 mm/¼ inch using a palette knife. Let set in a cool place.

Set the baking sheet on a damp tea towel on the work surface to prevent it from slipping. Hold a large kitchen knife in both hands and at a right angle to the chocolate. Drag the knife, across the set chocolate, towards you to make shards, shavings and curls of chocolate. Use a palette knife or fish slice to transfer the curls to another baking sheet or shallow box and chill until needed. Continue until all the chocolate has been shaved.

For a cheat's method, simply use a vegetable peeler to shave small curls off a bar of chocolate – the effect is not as dramatic, but just as delicious!

chocolate plastique

Chocolate plastique is an amazingly easy way of creating shapes. Using only chocolate and liquid glucose, you can effectively make a modelling dough with which to construct intricate flowers, butterflies and many other motifs. See page 28 for instructions.

making shapes with gum paste

When making flowers or other shapes to decorate a cake, I find that edible fine modelling paste such as gum or florist paste is the best thing to use. It generally comes in small packs and usually in white or ivory, although it is also available in a small range of colours. It is, however, easy to tint whichever shade you like using food colouring pastes. It is readily available at sugarcraft suppliers or online (see page 128).

Break off a small amount of paste at a time and keep the remainder tightly covered with clingfilm/plastic wrap to prevent it from drying out. Very lightly dust the work surface with icing/confectioners' sugar or rub a little groundnut or sunflower oil onto the area you are working in. Using a small rolling pin, roll out the gum paste as thinly as possible – roughly 1 mm/¹⁄₁₆ inch thick – and stamp out shapes or petals using cutters. Use your fingers to bend and shape the leaves or petals and then let dry on a tray or baking sheet covered with nonstick baking parchment. Repeat with the remaining gum paste. See page 52 for some beautiful gum-paste butterflies and flowers.

Decorate gum-paste shapes with finely piped dots of tinted royal icing left plain or adorned with sprinkles/nonpareils.

If you can't get hold of gum paste, you can use ready-to-roll royal or fondant icing, however it lacks the delicacy of gum paste and is not as easy to use. You will also find that it will not roll out as thinly and it takes longer to dry.

for birthdays

I love a simple lemon and poppy seed cake and I also love lemon and blueberries together, so this cake came about by putting those two loves together. Originally I wanted to bake the blueberries in the cake itself, but I found that cooking the berries to a purée and then using it as a filling really intensifies their flavour. A great cake for a summer afternoon tea party!

lemon poppy seed cake
with blueberries & lemon meringue buttercream

250 g/2 cups plain/
all-purpose flour

3 teaspoons baking powder

50 g/⅓ cup cornflour/cornstarch

a pinch of salt

150 g/10 tablespoons butter, soft

225 g/1 big cup (caster) sugar,
plus 5 tablespoons

4 large eggs, beaten

grated zest and juice of 3 lemons

1 tablespoon poppy seeds,
plus extra to serve

300 g/2½ cups blueberries,
plus extra to serve

icing/confectioners' sugar,
to dust

lemon meringue buttercream

4 tablespoons good lemon curd
(to make your own, see page 17)

1 teaspoon lemon extract

1 quantity Meringue Buttercream
(page 16, but follow the method
on this page)

*two 20-cm/8-inch springform
cake pans, greased and baselined
with greased baking parchment*

serves 10–12

Preheat the oven to 180°C (350°F) Gas 4.

Sift together the flour, baking powder, cornflour/cornstarch and salt.

Cream the butter and (caster) sugar in the bowl of a stand mixer until really pale and light – at least 3–4 minutes. Gradually add the beaten eggs to the creamed butter in 4 or 5 additions, mixing well between each addition and scraping down the bowl from time to time with a rubber spatula. Add the grated zest from 2 lemons and the poppy seeds and mix to incorporate.

Add the sifted dry ingredients to the bowl and mix until smooth. Add the juice from 1 lemon, mix well, then divide the mixture evenly between the prepared cake pans, scraping the mixture from the bowl using a rubber spatula. Spread level and bake on the middle shelf of the preheated oven for about 30 minutes or until golden, well risen and a skewer inserted in the middle comes out with a moist crumb.

While the cakes are baking, prepare a lemon syrup. Mix together 2 tablespoons of the extra (caster) sugar and the juice from a second lemon.

Remove the baked cakes from the oven and let cool in the pans for 3–4 minutes. Prick the cakes all over with a wooden skewer and pour the lemon syrup slowly over the tops. Let cool in the cake pans for a further 15 minutes, then carefully turn out onto a wire rack until cold.

Tip half the blueberries into a small saucepan, add the remaining 3 tablespoons of (caster) sugar and the juice from half the remaining lemon. Cook over low heat until the berries have burst and become juicy. Continue to cook until syrupy. Remove from the heat, add the remaining blueberries and leave until cold.

To make the lemon meringue buttercream, make the Meringue Buttercream as described on page 16, but replace the vanilla with grated zest from the remaining lemon, then add the lemon curd and extract and fold in gently.

Cut the cold cakes in half horizontally using a long serrated knife. Place one of the cake layers on a serving dish and spread one-quarter of the lemon meringue buttercream over it. Carefully spread one-third of the blueberry compote on top and cover with a second cake layer. Repeat this process twice. Finish with the last cake layer and the remaining lemon meringue buttercream. Scatter extra poppy seeds and blueberries on top and dust with icing/confectioners' sugar.

Here, a delicate white chocolate cake is layered and coated with rich chocolate ganache, then decorated with handmade chocolate roses, and if that wasn't enough, it's then dusted with gold. Making the chocolate plastique roses is much easier and more addictive than you'd imagine, and the final flourish of lustre and glitter makes this a cake for a very special occasion. You will find chocolate cigarillos at specialist cake suppliers and online but if you prefer you could coat the sides of the cake in grated white and dark/bittersweet chocolate.

gilded double chocolate cake
with chocolate roses

150 g/5 oz. white chocolate, chopped

1 quantity Basic Vanilla Cake (page 11, but follow the method on this page)

6 tablespoons apricot jam

1 quantity Chocolate Ganache (page 14)

edible gold glitter

edible gold lustre dust

chocolate cigarillos, to decorate

chocolate plastique roses

225 g/8 oz. dark/bittersweet chocolate (68–70% cocoa solids), chopped

140 g/4 tablespoons liquid glucose

three 20-cm/8-inch round cake pans, baselined with greased baking parchment

serves 10–12

To make the chocolate plastique roses, see instructions overleaf.

When you are ready to bake the cake, preheat the oven to 180°C (350°F) Gas 4.

Melt the white chocolate in a heatproof bowl set over a pan of barely simmering water. Do not let the base of the bowl touch the water.

Prepare the Basic Vanilla Cake mixture as described on page 11, then add the melted white chocolate to the cake mixture and stir to thoroughly combine. Divide the mixture evenly between the prepared pans and spread level with a palette knife. Bake the cakes on the middle shelf of the preheated oven for about 30 minutes or until a skewer inserted into the middle comes out clean. Let cool in the pans for 3–4 minutes, then turn out onto a wire rack to cool completely.

Gently heat the apricot jam to make it a little runnier, then strain it to get rid of any lumps.

Place one of the cake layers on a serving dish and spread a thin layer of the jam over it. Carefully spread 3–4 tablespoons of the Chocolate Ganache on top and cover with a second cake layer. Repeat this process. Lightly brush apricot jam over the whole cake, then cover all over with an even layer of ganache. Let set for 15–20 minutes before decorating.

Arrange the chocolate plastique roses on top of the cake and dust with edible gold glitter and lustre dust. Finally, gently press chocolate cigarillos all the way around the side of the cake.

(1)

(2)

To make the chocolate plastique roses, melt the chocolate in a heatproof bowl set over a pan of barely simmering water, stir until smooth, then let cool slightly. Gently warm the liquid glucose, then stir into the melted chocolate. Continue to stir until the mixture is smooth and pulls away from the side of the bowl. (1)

Spoon into a plastic freezer bag, let cool, then chill until required.

Lay a large sheet of clingfilm/plastic wrap on the work surface. Break off small nuggets of the chocolate plastique and roll between your hands into neat balls. They can vary slightly in size. Place on the clingfilm/plastic wrap. (2)

Cover with more clingfilm/plastic wrap and use your thumb to flatten each ball into a disc. (3)

Peel off and discard the top layer of film/wrap. Take one small chocolate disc and roll it into a spiral with your fingers. Take another disc and wrap this around the first spiral to make a petal shape. Pinch the bottom of the spiral (this is the base of the flower head) to create a cone shape. Repeat, adding more petals until the roses are the required size. Once you get the hang of this, you can become more creative and gently press the petals into points and curls. (4)

Let dry on baking parchment until ready to use.

(3)

By using the method below for making meringues, each of the 3 layers will be the same size once they are cooked, giving an elegant result to your meringue tower. If you prefer, you can pipe the meringue in a coil onto the baking parchment, starting from the middle of the circle and working your way outwards in a spiral. I have used summer berries and passionfruit for the filling, but peaches and blackcurrants, baked spiced plums or even lightly stewed apples and blackberries would work deliciously.

meringue cloud cake
with berries, passionfruit & pistachios

350 g/1¾ cups caster/superfine sugar

175 g/¾ cup egg whites (about 4–5 large)

a pinch of salt

the seeds from 1 vanilla pod/bean or 1 teaspoon vanilla extract

1 teaspoon white wine vinegar

75 g/½ cup unsalted pistachios, chopped, plus a little extra to decorate

filling

300 ml/1¼ cups double/heavy cream

200 ml/¾ cup Greek yogurt

250 g/2 cups strawberries, hulled and halved or quartered

200 g/1⅔ cups raspberries

125 g/1 cup blueberries

125 g/1 cup blackberries

juice and seeds from 2 passionfruit

topping

small handful each of strawberries, raspberries, blueberries and blackberrries

icing/confectioners' sugar, to dust

3 sheets of baking parchment

3 baking sheets

serves 8

Preheat the oven to 200°C (400°F) Gas 6.

Draw a 20-cm/8-inch circle on each sheet of baking parchment. Flip the paper over and lay one on each of the baking sheets – you should be able to see the circle through the paper.

Tip the sugar into a small roasting pan and place on the middle shelf of the preheated oven for about 5 minutes or until hot to the touch. When the sugar is ready, turn the oven temperature down to 110°C (225°F) Gas ¼.

Meanwhile, whisk the egg whites and salt in the bowl of a stand mixer until frothy. With the motor running on low speed, tip the hot sugar onto the egg whites in one go. Turn the speed up to medium–high and whisk for about 8 minutes or until the meringue is very stiff, white and cold. Add the vanilla and vinegar and mix again for a further minute until thoroughly combined.

Spoon the meringue onto the prepared baking sheets in equal quantities and, using a palette knife, spread evenly into the outlined circles. Scatter chopped pistachios over each meringue. Bake in the preheated oven for 1¼ hours or until the top and underside are crisp and the insides are still marshmallowy. You may need to swap the baking sheets around the shelves halfway through cooking so that all the meringues cook evenly. Remove from the oven and let cool on the baking sheets.

To make the filling, whip the cream in a stand mixer or with an electric hand whisk until it will just hold a peak, then add the yogurt and fold in using a large metal spoon.

In a large bowl, lightly mix the summer berries with the passionfruit.

Peel the paper away from one meringue layer and place the meringue on a serving dish. Top with half the cream mixture, spreading it evenly with a palette knife. Scatter half the mixed fruit over the top, then cover with a second meringue layer. Spread the remaining cream mixture, then the mixed fruit over it. Top with the third meringue layer, pressing the layers gently together.

Arrange the whole berries on top, decorate with a few more chopped pistachios and dust lightly with icing/confectioners' sugar. Serve immediately.

This is my take on a much-loved classic. This time I have filled and covered the deep, red cake layers in a cream cheese frosting, but it's equally good with a billowing cloud of marshmallow frosting. There's no need for any wildly creative artistic streak or even a steady hand for the chocolate squiggles – in fact, the more swirly and free-style the better!

red velvet layer cake

1 quantity Basic Vanilla Cake (page 11, but follow the method on this page)

2 big tablespoons cocoa powder

1 teaspoon red food colouring paste (Ruby or Christmas Red)

to decorate

200 g/6½ oz. dark/bittersweet or semisweet chocolate, finely chopped

1½ quantities Cream Cheese Frosting (page 14)

three 20-cm/8-inch round cake pans, greased and baselined with greased baking parchment

disposable piping bag

2 baking sheets, lined with nonstick baking parchment

serves 10

Preheat the oven to 180°C (350°F) Gas 4.

Prepare the Basic Vanilla Cake mixture as described on page 11, but add the cocoa powder to the dry ingredients and whisk the red food colouring paste into the buttermilk before mixing.

Divide the mixture evenly between the prepared pans and spread level with a palette knife. Bake the cakes on the middle shelf of the preheated oven for about 20–25 minutes or until a skewer inserted into the middle comes out clean. Let cool in the pans for 3–4 minutes, then turn out onto a wire rack to cool completely.

To make the dark chocolate squiggles, melt the chocolate in a heatproof bowl set over a pan of barely simmering water. Do not let the base of the bowl touch the water. Stir until smooth, then let cool slightly.

Spoon the melted chocolate into the piping bag and snip the end to a fine point. Pipe elaborate swirls and squiggles over the baking parchment. Refrigerate until completely set and firm.

When you are ready to assemble the cake, place one of the cake layers on a serving dish and spread about 3 tablespoons of the Cream Cheese Frosting over it. Carefully place a second cake layer on top and spread another 3 tablespoons of frosting over it. Finally, top with the last cake layer and gently press the cake layers together.

Spread the remaining frosting over the top and side of the cake using a palette knife.

Remove the chocolate squiggles from the fridge and, using a palette knife, carefully lift them off the paper. Gently press into the frosting around the side of the cake.

The ultimate chocoholic's treat, with a triple hit of the good stuff in the form of chocolate cake, chocolate frosting and chocolate truffles. You could, if you were of a mind to, make your own chocolate truffles, but there's something rather lovely about a tray of these little cakes each topped with a decadent, varied truffle selection. Make the cake bases for these indulgent squares the day before you plan to cut and frost them.

mini chocolate truffle cakes

1 quantity Basic Chocolate Cake
(page 11)
1 quantity Rum or Brandy Syrup
(page 17)
1 quantity Chocolate Cream
Frosting (page 15)

to decorate
100 g/⅔ cup finely chopped
mixed nuts, toasted
100 g/⅔ cup chocolate
vermicelli/jimmies
36 assorted chocolate truffles

*23 x 33 x 5-cm/9 x 13 x 2-inch
baking pan, greased and lined
with greased baking parchment*

*piping bag, fitted with a star
nozzle/tip*

makes 12

Preheat the oven to 180°C (350°F) Gas 4.

Prepare the Basic Chocolate Cake mixture as described on page 11, then transfer to the prepared baking pan and spread level with a palette knife. Bake on the middle shelf of the preheated oven for about 40 minutes or until a skewer inserted into the middle comes out clean. Let cool in the pan for 3–4 minutes, then turn out onto a wire rack to cool completely.

Brush the Rum or Brandy Syrup liberally over the top of the cooled cake. Cover the cake in clingfilm/plastic wrap and set aside for a couple of hours or until the next day, by which point the cake will be easier to frost.

Pour the chopped nuts and chocolate vermicelli/jimmies onto separate plates.

Trim the edges of the cold cake. Cut in half horizontally using a long serrated knife. Place one of the cake layers on a board and spread 3–4 tablespoons of the Chocolate Cream Frosting over it. Cover with the second cake layer.

Cut the cake into 12 even cubes. Using a palette knife, spread chocolate cream frosting over the sides of each cake. Press the sides in either the chopped nuts or the chocolate vermicelli/jimmies until evenly coated.

Spoon the remaining chocolate cream frosting into the piping bag and pipe small rosettes on top of each cake. Arrange 3 chocolate truffles on top of each cake just before serving.

Here's a rich, towering chocolate cake that's filled with my take on the classic German Chocolate Cake frosting (which is nothing whatsoever to do with Germany but in fact a classic American cake created to make use of a particular brand of baking chocolate). The combination of toasted coconut, pecans, slightly salty caramel sauce and dark chocolate ganache is really quite heady!

german chocolate cake

1 quantity Basic Chocolate Cake (page 11, but follow the method on this page)
3 teaspoons instant coffee granules dissolved in 2 teaspoons boiling water
1 quantity Chocolate Ganache (page 14)

'german chocolate' filling
150 g/1 cup shelled pecans
150 g/1¾ cups desiccated coconut
200 ml/¾ cup double/heavy cream
200 g/1 cup packed light brown soft sugar
3 large egg yolks
50 g/3 tablespoons butter
1 teaspoon vanilla extract
½ teaspoon salt

three 20-cm/8-inch round cake pans, greased and baselined with greased baking parchment

piping bag, fitted with a star nozzle/tip

serves 10–12

Preheat the oven to 180°C (350°F) Gas 4.

Prepare the Basic Chocolate Cake mixture as described on page 11, adding the coffee with the melted chocolate. Divide the mixture evenly between the prepared pans and spread level with a palette knife. Bake the cakes on the middle shelf of the preheated oven for about 25 minutes or until a skewer inserted into the middle comes out clean. Let cool in the pans for 3–4 minutes, then turn out onto a wire rack to cool completely. Leave the oven on.

Tip the pecans onto a baking sheet and toast in the preheated oven for 4–5 minutes. Roughly chop the pecans and let cool.

Spread the desiccated coconut onto a baking sheet and toast in the preheated oven for 3 minutes, or until lightly golden.

Put the cream, sugar, egg yolks and butter in a medium saucepan over low heat. Cook gently, stirring constantly, for about 7 minutes or until the mixture is smooth and has thickened. Remove from the heat, add the vanilla, salt, toasted pecans and all but 2 tablespoons of the toasted coconut and stir to combine.

Place one of the cake layers on a serving dish, spread one-third of the coconut mixture over it and cover with another cake layer. Repeat this process. Finish with the last cake layer and top with the remaining coconut frosting. Spread smooth with a palette knife.

Spread a thin layer of the Chocolate Ganache all around the side of the cake using a palette knife. Let set for about 30 minutes.

Now spread a second layer of ganache around the side of the cake, making it as smooth as possible. Spoon the remaining ganache into the piping bag and pipe rosettes around the top edge of the cake. Scatter the reserved toasted coconut over the rosettes.

To achieve perfect results for this cake you will need to make use of a ruler or tape measure, and then it's just a simple construction number rather like building a brick wall – though much tastier! I also strongly recommend that you bake the cake the day before you want to serve it, as this will make it easier to cut and assemble.

white & dark chocolate checkerboard cake

75 g/2½ oz. white chocolate, chopped

75 g/2½ oz. dark/semisweet chocolate, chopped

1 quantity Basic Vanilla Cake (see page 11, but follow the method on this page)

½ quantity Chocolate Cream Frosting (page 15)

1 quantity Meringue Buttercream (page 16)

two 20 x 30 x 4-cm/8 x 12 x 1¾-inch baking pans, greased and lined with greased baking parchment

cocktail sticks/toothpicks

2 disposable piping bags

serves 8–10

Start making the cake the day before you want to serve it.

Preheat the oven to 180°C (350°F) Gas 4.

Melt the white and dark/semisweet chocolates in separate heatproof bowls set over pans of barely simmering water, stirring until smooth. Do not let the base of the bowl touch the water.

Prepare the Basic Vanilla Cake mixture as described on page 11, then weigh it and divide it equally between 2 bowls. Add the melted white chocolate to one bowl and the dark/semisweet chocolate to the other. Mix until thoroughly combined, then transfer each mixture to a separate prepared baking pan. Spread level with a palette knife.

Bake the cakes on the middle shelf of the preheated oven for about 30 minutes or until a skewer inserted into the middle comes out clean. Let cool in the pans for 3–4 minutes, then turn out onto a wire rack to cool completely. Wrap the cold cakes in clingfilm/plastic wrap and set aside until the following day.

When you are ready to assemble the cake, follow the instructions overleaf.

(1)

Lay the white chocolate cake on the work surface and, using a palette knife, spread a thin layer of Chocolate Cream Frosting over it. Lay the dark chocolate cake on top. (**1**)

Using a long serrated knife, trim the edges of the cake to give neat, straight sides. With the long side of the cake nearest to you, use a ruler to divide the cake into 6 strips of equal thickness. Use cocktail sticks/toothpicks as a guide to ensure that you cut the strips evenly. (**2**)

Take the 3 strips on the left-hand side of you and remove the middle one. Flip it over and spread chocolate cream thinly over the sides. Put it back in its place, upside down, so that the 3 strips are starting to show a checkerboard pattern. Press them gently and neatly together. Spread a thin layer of chocolate cream over the top of them.

Lay the remaining 3 strips alternately on top, flipping the middle one over again and spreading chocolate cream thinly between each strip. (**3**)

Spread a thin layer of chocolate cream over the whole cake, transfer to a serving dish and refrigerate for 10 minutes. (**4**)

Remove the cake from the fridge and cover it evenly with Meringue Buttercream. Spoon the remaining chocolate cream and meringue buttercream separately into the piping bags and snip the ends to fine points. Pipe alternate beads of frosting around the top edges of the cake.

If a lemon meringue pie was to become a cake, then this is probably what it would taste like, only better. A light coconut cake is sandwiched with tangy lime curd and enveloped in marshmallow frosting before being topped with shavings of toasted fresh coconut.

coconut heaven cake
with lime curd & marshmallow frosting

250 g/2 cups plain/all-purpose flour

3 teaspoons baking powder

a pinch of salt

175 g/1½ sticks butter, soft

250 g/1¼ cups (caster) sugar

4 large eggs, beaten

3 tablespoons coconut cream

juice and finely grated zest of 2 limes

50 g/½ cup desiccated coconut

3–4 tablespoons Malibu (optional)

1 fresh coconut

1 quantity Marshmallow Frosting (page 16)

lime curd

6 large egg yolks

juice of 4 limes and finely grated zest of 2

175 g/¾ cup (caster) sugar

a pinch of salt

75 g/5 tablespoons butter, diced

three 20-cm/8-inch round cake pans, greased and baselined with greased baking parchment

baking sheet, lined with baking parchment

serves 10

Preheat the oven to 180°C (350°F) Gas 4.

Sift together the flour, baking powder and salt.

Cream the butter and sugar in the bowl of a stand mixer until really pale and light – at least 3–4 minutes. Gradually add the beaten eggs to the creamed butter in 4 or 5 additions, mixing well between each addition and scraping down the bowl from time to time with a rubber spatula.

Add the sifted dry ingredients to the cake mixture alternately with the coconut cream and lime juice. Mix until smooth, then add the grated lime zest and desiccated coconut. Divide the mixture evenly between the prepared cake pans, scraping the mixture from the bowl using a rubber spatula. Spread level and bake on the middle shelf of the preheated oven for about 30 minutes or until a skewer inserted into the middle comes out clean. Leave the oven on.

Let the cakes cool in the pans for 3–4 minutes, then turn out onto a wire rack. Drizzle the Malibu over each cake (if using), then set aside until cold.

Remove the fresh coconut from the shell and shave the flesh into strips using a vegetable peeler. Arrange on the prepared baking sheet and toast in the hot oven for 3–5 minutes or until lightly browned and starting to curl at the edges. Remove from the oven and let cool.

To make the lime curd, combine the egg yolks, lime juice, sugar, salt and butter in a medium heatproof bowl set over a pan of simmering water. Do not let the base of the bowl touch the water. Whisk the mixture to combine, then stir constantly for about 5–7 minutes until thickened and the curd will coat the back of a wooden spoon.

Remove from the heat and pass through a fine nylon sieve/strainer into a bowl. Add the lime zest, stir until smooth and cover the surface of the curd with clingfilm/plastic wrap to prevent a skin from forming. Let cool completely, then refrigerate until firm.

To assemble the cake, place one of the cake layers on a serving dish, spread half the cold, firm lime curd over it and cover with a second cake layer. Repeat this process. Finish with the last cake layer and gently press the cake layers together.

Spread the Marshmallow Frosting evenly over the top and side of the cake using a palette knife. Pile the cooled, toasted coconut shavings on top.

This recipe takes my basic vanilla cake recipe from page 11 and shakes it up a bit. Adding grated chocolate to the mixture means that you get just a delicate chocolate hit. The caramel hazelnuts are easy once you get the hang of them and really do make a slice of this cake a talking point – however, you could just as easily scatter the top of the cake with extra praline and it would be no less delicious.

hazelnut praline chocolate cake

175 g/1⅓ cups blanched hazelnuts
1 quantity Basic Vanilla Cake (see page 11, but follow the method on this page)
50 g/1¾ oz. dark/bittersweet chocolate, coarsely grated
100 g/½ cup (caster) sugar
1 quantity Hazelnut Liqueur Syrup (page 17)
5–6 tablespoons Chocolate Ganache (page 14)
1 quantity Chocolate Fudge Frosting (page 15)

two 23-cm/9-inch round cake pans, greased and baselined with greased baking parchment

2 baking sheets, oiled

serves 10

Preheat the oven to 180°C (350°F) Gas 4.

Tip the hazelnuts onto a baking sheet and toast in the preheated oven for 5 minutes. Leave the oven on. Let the hazelnuts cool completely, then put about 75 g/½ cup of them in a food processor and whizz until finely ground. Reserve the remaining hazelnuts until you make the praline.

Prepare the Basic Vanilla Cake mixture as described on page 11, then fold the ground hazelnuts and grated chocolate into it and stir until thoroughly incorporated. Divide the mixture evenly between the prepared cake pans, scraping the mixture from the bowl using a rubber spatula. Spread level and bake on the middle shelf of the preheated oven for about 35 minutes or until a skewer inserted into the middle comes out clean.

Let the cakes cool in the pans for 3–4 minutes, then turn out onto a wire rack to cool completely.

To make the praline and candied hazelnuts, half-fill the kitchen sink with cold water, ready for later. Put the sugar and 1–2 tablespoons water in a small, heavy-based saucepan set over low heat. Cook to completely dissolve the sugar. Bring to the boil and cook until the syrup turns to an amber-coloured caramel. Remove from the heat and plunge the bottom of the pan into the sink of cold water. Quickly tip half of the reserved hazelnuts into the pan and stir to coat in the caramel. Using a slotted spoon, scoop the hazelnuts out of the pan (leaving the excess caramel in the pan) and onto one of the oiled baking sheets in a block.

Push a cocktail stick/toothpick into each of the remaining hazelnuts and one at a time dip them into the caramel so that each nut has a long caramel tail. Let harden on the second oiled baking sheet. You may need to gently warm the caramel over a low heat halfway through. When the block of caramel nuts is completely cold and hardened, whizz in a food processor until you get finely chopped praline.

Place one of the cake layers on a serving dish and brush some Hazelnut Liqueur Syrup over it. Spread 3–4 tablespoons of the Chocolate Ganache over the top and scatter all the chopped praline over it. Cover with the second cake layer. Brush more of the hazelnut liqueur syrup over it and let soak in for 5 minutes.

Spread the Chocolate Fudge Frosting evenly over the top and side of the cake using a palette knife. Decorate the cake with the whole caramel hazelnuts, stuck in place with a neat dollop of chocolate ganache.

Tiramisù is one of my all-time favourite desserts, so I had to include it here in cake form. The cake is as light as a feather and filled with a white chocolate and Marsala mascarpone cream with a sprinkling of grated dark chocolate between each layer. You will need to bake the cake the day before you want to serve it.

tempting tiramisù cake

1 quantity Whisked Almond Cake (page 12)

75 g/2½ oz. dark/bittersweet chocolate, grated, plus extra to decorate

100 g/3½ oz. amaretti biscuits/cookies, crushed

coffee syrup

150 ml/⅔ cup hot espresso or strong rich coffee

1 tablespoon demerera sugar

25 g/1 oz. dark/bittersweet chocolate, finely chopped

white chocolate mascarpone filling

4 large egg yolks

50 g/¼ cup (caster) sugar

125 ml/½ cup Marsala

a pinch of salt

100 g/3½ oz. white chocolate, chopped

500 g/2 cups mascarpone

two 23-cm/9-inch springform cake pans, greased and baselined with greased baking parchment

serves 10–12

Start making the cake the day before you want to serve it.

Preheat the oven to 180°C (350°F) Gas 4.

Prepare the Whisked Almond Cake mixture as described on page 12, then divide evenly between the prepared cake pans and spread level with a palette knife. Bake on the middle shelf of the preheated oven for about 20 minutes or until a skewer inserted into the middle comes out clean. Let cool in the pan for 3–4 minutes, then turn out onto a wire rack to cool completely. Wrap the cold cakes in clingfilm/plastic wrap and set aside until the following day.

When you are ready to assemble the cake, make the coffee syrup. Pour the hot coffee into a bowl, add the sugar and chocolate and stir until smooth and the chocolate has completely melted.

To make the white chocolate mascarpone filling, half-fill the kitchen sink with cold water, ready for later. Put the egg yolks, sugar, Marsala and salt in a medium heatproof ceramic or glass bowl set over a pan of simmering water. Do not let the base of the bowl touch the water. Whisk with a balloon whisk for about 5 minutes until the mixture is hot to the touch, very thick and has tripled in volume. Remove from the heat and plunge the bottom of the pan into the sink of cold water. Whisk until the mixture is cold.

Melt the white chocolate in a heatproof bowl set over a pan of barely simmering water, stirring until smooth. Do not let the base of the bowl touch the water.

Beat the mascarpone until smooth, then fold it into the cold egg mixture together with the melted white chocolate.

Cut the cold cakes in half horizontally using a long serrated knife. Fit one of the cake layers carefully in the bottom of one of the springform cake pans. Brush one-third of the coffee syrup over it, spread 3–4 tablespoons of the white chocolate mascarpone filling on top, then finish with an even scattering of grated dark/bittersweet chocolate. Cover with a second cake layer. Repeat this process twice. Cover with clingfilm/plastic wrap and refrigerate for at least 2 hours.

Pop the cake out of the springform cake pan and onto a serving dish. Spread the remaining white chocolate mascarpone filling evenly over the top and side of the cake using a palette knife. Press the crushed amaretti biscuits/cookies all around the side of the cake and decorate the top with extra grated dark/bittersweet chocolate.

for kids

I have my fabulous assistant Rachel to thank for the name of this cake – Dazzle Drops were chocolate treats much loved by her and her brother when they were little. Decorate your dazzle drops with sprinkles in a single colour for a sophisticated look, or in a dazzling selection of shades for a more dramatic effect.

chocolate dazzle drop cake

1 quantity Basic Chocolate Cake
(page 11)
1 quantity Chocolate Meringue
Buttercream (page 17)

dazzle drops

100 g/3½ oz. dark/bittersweet
chocolate, chopped
100 g/3½ oz. white chocolate,
chopped
100 g/3½ oz. milk chocolate,
chopped
assorted coloured sugar
sprinkles/nonpareils

*two 23-cm/9-inch round cake
pans, greased and baselined with
greased baking parchment*

*2 large baking sheets, lined with
(uncreased!) baking parchment*

*piping bag, fitted with a star
nozzle/tip*

serves 12

Preheat the oven to 180°C (350°F) Gas 4.

Prepare the Basic Chocolate Cake mixture as described on page 11. Divide the mixture evenly between the prepared pans and spread level with a palette knife. Bake the cakes on the middle shelf of the preheated oven for 25 minutes or until a skewer inserted into the middle comes out clean. Let cool in the pans for 3–4 minutes, then turn out onto a wire rack to cool completely.

While the cakes are cooling, make the chocolate dazzle drops. Melt the 3 types of chocolate in separate heatproof bowls set over pans of barely simmering water, stirring until smooth. Do not let the base of the bowl touch the water.

Dazzle drops look all the more dazzling with a vibrant and contrasting selection of coloured sprinkles/nonpareils. (**1**)

Using a teaspoon, dollop small spoonfuls of dark/bittersweet, white and milk chocolate onto the prepared baking sheets. They can vary in size, and be aware that they will spread slightly as they settle. Continue until you have used up all the melted chocolate. (**2**)

Scatter sprinkles/nonpareils over all the molten chocolate drops and let set until hard. (**3**)

To assemble the cake, place one of the cake layers on a serving dish and spread an even layer of Chocolate Meringue Buttercream over it. Top with the second cake layer and gently press the cakes together. Spread almost all the remaining chocolate meringue buttercream evenly over the top and side of the cake using a palette knife.

Spoon the remaining chocolate meringue buttercream into the piping bag and pipe shell shapes around the top edge of the cake and small rosettes around the bottom edge.

Press the chocolate dazzle drops over the top and side of the cake to cover.

This cake with its garden of summer blooms and fluttering butterflies would be just the ticket for a birthday party or even a christening tea. You will need to prepare the butterflies and flowers for this cake at least 24 hours in advance. If you are using gum paste, you will find that it is much easier to work with and it will dry much quicker than ready-made royal icing. I have kept the decoration on the butterflies and flowers very simple, but you could always pipe more intricate patterns using royal icing in contrasting colours.

summer garden cake

200 g/7 oz. white gum paste
assorted food colouring pastes
icing/confectioners' sugar,
to dust
1 quantity Royal Icing (page 15)
1 quantity Basic Vanilla Cake
(page 11)
1 quantity Meringue Buttercream
(page 16)
3 tablespoons good lemon curd
(to make your own, see page 17),
strawberry jam or raspberry jam
*assorted butterfly- and flower-
shaped cutters*
*three 20-cm/8-inch round cake
pans, greased and baselined with
greased baking parchment*
disposable piping bags

serves 12

Make the butterflies and flowers at least 24 hours before you bake the cake. See page 20 for instructions on how to make them. Use the gum paste tinted in whichever colours you like using food colouring pastes, and make the butterflies and flowers in varying sizes and colours.

Once the basic butterfly and flower shapes have dried sufficiently, decorate them with royal icing. Make up small batches of icing in various shades to suit the colour palette you have chosen and spoon them into disposable piping bags. Snip the ends to fine points and pipe decorative patterns over the butterflies and flowers. Let dry for at least a couple of hours before using to decorate the finished cake.

When you are ready to make the cake, preheat the oven to 180°C (350°F) Gas 4.

Prepare the Basic Vanilla Cake mixture as described on page 11. Divide the mixture evenly between the prepared pans and spread level with a palette knife. Bake the cakes on the middle shelf of the preheated oven for about 25 minutes or until a skewer inserted into the middle comes out clean. Let cool in the pans for 3–4 minutes, then turn out onto a wire rack to cool completely.

Meanwhile, use a little food colouring paste of your choice to tint the Meringue Buttercream – stir it in gradually until you get the pale shade you like.

To assemble the cake, place one of the cake layers on a serving dish. Spread 2–3 tablespoons of Meringue Buttercream over it, carefully spread half the lemon curd evenly over the top and cover with a second cake layer. Gently press the cakes together. Repeat this process. Spread the remaining meringue buttercream evenly over the top and side of the cake using a palette knife. Refrigerate for 30 minutes.

When you are ready to serve the cake, decorate with the butterflies and flowers, pressing them gently into the buttercream.

No cake book would be complete without at least one recipe for cupcakes. And no party would be complete without some pretty nostalgic bunting strung from pillar to post. So here I've combined the two to make homemade bunting cupcakes. I've used rubber stamps with picture shapes to decorate the bunting triangles, but you could try spelling out names or simply using patterned paper. Rubber stamps in alphabets, numbers and shapes are widely available in good artist supply stores and online, and ink pads now come in a dazzling rainbow of colours.

cute cupcakes with bunting

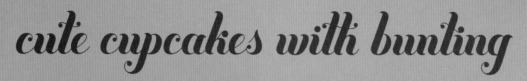

1 quantity Basic Vanilla Cake (page 11)

1 quantity Basic Chocolate Cake (page 11)

1 quantity Meringue Buttercream (page 16)

1 quantity Chocolate Meringue Buttercream (page 17)

assorted coloured sugar sprinkles/nonpareils

two 12-hole muffin pans, lined with pretty paper cupcake cases

paper or card for making bunting

fine ribbon or coloured string

glue

2 large piping bags, fitted with star nozzles/tips

wooden skewers or thin sticks

makes 24

Preheat the oven to 180°C (350°F) Gas 4.

Prepare the Basic Vanilla Cake mixture as described on page 11. Divide the mixture evenly between 12 cupcake cases and bake on the middle shelf of the preheated oven for about 20 minutes or until a skewer inserted into the middle comes out clean. Let cool in the pans for 3–4 minutes, then turn out onto a wire rack to cool completely.

Prepare the Basic Chocolate Cake mixture as described on page 11 and bake as above.

Meanwhile, make the bunting. Using plain or pretty patterned paper or card, cut out small, equal-sized diamond shapes – whatever size and however many you like – and fold them in half to make double-sided triangles. Leave them plain or draw/stamp pictures on them. Take a length of fine ribbon or string and slip the folded triangles over it at regular intervals. Stick each folded triangle shut with a dab of glue.

Spoon the Meringue Buttercream into one piping bag and pipe generous swirls of frosting onto each cold vanilla cupcake. Scatter sprinkles/nonpareils over the top. Repeat this process with the Chocolate Meringue Buttercream and chocolate cupcakes.

Arrange the cupcakes on pretty cake stands. Work out where you want the bunting to go, then tie the lengths of prepared bunting to wooden skewers or thin sticks and push gently into the cupcakes so that the flags flutter above the cakes.

I don't think I know a child that can resist a pile of colourful mini meringues – and these ones are sure to bring smiles to little faces at any birthday party. I have decorated half of the meringues with coloured sugar sprinkles and marbled the rest with red or blue food colouring. No matter how many you make or in which colours, these meringues will disappear in a wink of an eye.

super-duper disco meringues

meringue mixture

300 g/1½ cups caster/superfine sugar

150 g/⅔ cup egg whites (about 4 large)

a pinch of salt

to decorate

2 food colouring pastes in colours of your choice

assorted coloured sugar sprinkles/nonpareils

600 ml/2½ cups double/heavy cream

clean craft brush

3 large piping bags, fitted with plain and/or star nozzles/tips

3 large baking sheets, lined with baking parchment

makes about 30

Preheat the oven to 200°C (400°F) Gas 6.

To make the meringue mixture, tip the sugar into a small roasting pan and place on the middle shelf of the preheated oven for about 5 minutes or until hot to the touch. When the sugar is ready, turn the oven temperature down to 110°C (225°F) Gas ¼.

Meanwhile, whisk the egg whites in the bowl of a stand mixer until frothy. With the motor running on low speed, tip the hot sugar onto the egg whites in one go. Turn the speed up to medium–high and whisk for about 8 minutes or until the meringue is very stiff, white and cold. Divide the mixture between 3 bowls.

Using a clean craft brush, paint 3 fine, straight lines of one food colouring paste on the inside of a piping bag, going from the nozzle/tip toward the opening. Fill the bag with one-third of the meringue mixture. Pipe small (3–4-cm/1¼–1½-inch) meringues onto a prepared baking sheet in spirals. Try to make them all roughly the same size.

Repeat this process with another third of the meringue mixture, using a different colour in the piping bag.

Fill the third piping bag with the remaining meringue mixture and pipe plain, uncoloured swirls of meringue onto the third baking sheet.

Scatter sprinkles/nonpareils lightly over the plain meringues. Bake all the meringues in the preheated oven for about 40–45 minutes. You may need to swap the baking sheets around the shelves halfway through cooking so that all the meringues cook evenly. Remove from the oven and let cool on the baking sheets.

Whip the cream until just stiff, then spoon into one of the cleaned piping bags. Pipe the cream onto the base of half of the meringues. Sandwich with another meringue and arrange on a serving dish.

1

2

3

I won't lie and tell you that this is a cinch to make. The polka-dot collars require patience and a cool, but not too cool kitchen – do not attempt this if your kitchen is steaming hot. However, when all's said and done, this is a real crowd pleaser!

chocolate polka-dot tower

1 quantity Basic Chocolate Cake
(page 11)

1 quantity Chocolate Fudge
Frosting (page 15)

100 g/3½ oz. white chocolate,
chopped

100 g/3½ oz. milk chocolate,
chopped

300 g/10 oz. dark/semisweet
chocolate, chopped

assorted coloured, candy-coated
chocolate drops

*two 20-cm/8-inch round cake
pans, greased and lined with
greased baking parchment*

*15-cm/6-inch round cake pan,
greased and lined with greased
baking parchment*

*10-cm/4-inch round cake pan,
greased and lined with greased
baking parchment*

3 sheets of baking parchment

2 disposable piping bags

serves 10–12

Preheat the oven to 180°C (350°F) Gas 4.

Prepare the Basic Chocolate Cake mixture as described on page 11. Divide the mixture evenly between the prepared pans, filling them two-thirds full, and spread level with a palette knife. Bake on the middle shelf of the preheated oven for about 20–30 minutes, depending on their size, until a skewer inserted into the middle comes out clean. Let cool in the pans for 3–4 minutes, then turn out onto a wire rack to cool completely.

Spread 3–4 tablespoons of Chocolate Fudge Frosting over one of the 2 largest cakes, then sandwich with the other largest cake. Spread an even layer of the frosting over the top and side of the cake using a palette knife. Cut the medium cake in half horizontally using a long serrated knife, spread 3 tablespoons of the frosting over it and sandwich with the other layer. Spread frosting over the top and side. Cover the smaller cake with frosting.

Measure the circumference and height of each cake. Draw a rectangle slightly longer and slightly higher than each cake on the sheets of baking parchment. Flip the paper over. There's no need to cut along the lines yet.

Melt the white and milk chocolates in separate heatproof

bowls set over pans of barely simmering water, stirring until smooth. Do not let the base of the bowl touch the water. Spoon each melted chocolate into separate piping bags and snip the ends to fine points. Pipe dots of varying sizes over each sheet of paper within the lines. Let set completely. (**1**)

Melt the dark/semisweet chocolate as above and let cool to room temperature. Carefully, so as not to disturb the dots, spread the melted chocolate within the measured rectangle, completely covering the dots. Try to make the bottom edge quite straight but don't worry if the top is a little wonky. Repeat with the other 2 sheets of paper. (**2**)

Let cool until almost set. It's a fine line between being too hard and too soft – it should be pliable but no longer melted. Trim the paper near the bottom line. Take the largest strip and wrap it around the largest cake, chocolate side to the cake. Completely encase the cake and carefully peel away the paper. Hold it in place until you are sure that it is firmly stuck to the cake. (**3**)

Repeat with the other cakes. Let set completely, then stack the cakes one on top of another. Scatter the chocolate drops between the chocolate collar and the cake just before serving.

If a Snickers bar was to become a cake, then this is what it would taste like. The salted caramel popcorn topping is possibly a tad indulgent with its chocolate chips, mini marshmallows and peanuts, but I would never suggest that you eat this every afternoon – this is a celebration cake after all. You could leave out the popcorn if you like, but where's the fun in that?

peanut butter & chocolate cake
with salted caramel popcorn

350 g/2⅔ cups plain/all-purpose flour

3 teaspoons baking powder

1 teaspoon bicarbonate of/ baking soda

150 g/10 tablespoons butter, soft

100 g/½ cup crunchy peanut butter

350 g/1¾ cups (caster) sugar

4 large eggs, lightly beaten

1 teaspoon vanilla extract

250 ml/1 cup buttermilk, room temperature

125 g/¾ cup chocolate chips

½ quantity Chocolate Fudge Frosting (page 15)

peanut butter frosting

200 g/6½ oz. cream cheese

50 g/3½ tablespoons butter, soft

75 g/⅓ cup peanut butter

1 teaspoon vanilla extract

4 tablespoons maple syrup

salted caramel popcorn

50 g/¼ cup (caster) sugar

25 g/2 tablespoons butter

50 g/2 cups plain popcorn (popped weight)

50 g/⅓ cup roasted peanuts

50 g/⅓ cup chocolate chips

50 g/⅔ cup mini marshmallows

three 20-cm/8-inch round cake pans, greased and baselined with greased baking parchment

serves 12

Preheat the oven to 180°C (350°F) Gas 4.

Sift together the flour, baking powder and bicarbonate of/baking soda.

Cream the butter, peanut butter and sugar in the bowl of a stand mixer until really pale and light – at least 3–4 minutes. Gradually add the beaten eggs to the creamed butter in 4 or 5 additions, mixing well between each addition and scraping down the bowl from time to time with a rubber spatula. Add the vanilla and mix to incorporate.

Gradually add the sifted dry ingredients to the cake mixture alternately with the buttermilk. Mix until smooth, then fold in the chocolate chips. Divide the mixture evenly between the prepared cake pans, scraping the mixture from the bowl using a rubber spatula. Spread level with a palette knife and bake on the middle shelf of the preheated oven for about 20–25 minutes or until a skewer inserted into the middle comes out clean. Let the cakes cool in the pans for 3–4 minutes, then turn out onto a wire rack to cool completely.

To make the peanut butter frosting, beat the cream cheese until smooth. Add the butter, peanut butter, vanilla and maple syrup and beat again until creamy.

To make the salted caramel popcorn, put the sugar and 1 tablespoon water in a small, heavy-based saucepan over low heat and dissolve the sugar without stirring. Once dissolved, increase the heat and continue to cook until the syrup turns into an amber-coloured caramel. Take the pan off the heat and add the butter, swirling to make a smooth butterscotch. Quickly pour the butterscotch over the popcorn and stir well so that it starts to stick together in clumps. Add the peanuts (chopped, if you prefer), chocolate chips and marshmallows.

Place one of the cake layers on a serving dish and spread half the peanut butter frosting over it. Carefully spread one-third of the Chocolate Fudge Frosting over that. Cover with a second cake layer. Repeat this process, finishing with the last cake layer and the remaining chocolate fudge frosting on top of that. Pile the salted caramel popcorn on top just before serving.

Sometimes smaller is better, and these little gems of cake are no exception. They are perfect for a kids' party, as they are just enough for little hands and they can be packaged into pretty boxes to take away as favours. They do need to be prepared a day in advance, so plan accordingly. However, that does mean you will have less to worry about on the day of the party!

mini iced gem cakes

1 quantity Basic Vanilla Cake
(page 11)
4 tablespoons strawberry jam
1 quantity Meringue Buttercream
(page 16)
assorted food colouring pastes
coloured sugar strands/jimmies
assorted, coloured gummy
sweets/candies

20 x 30 x 4-cm/8 x 12 x
1¾-inch baking pan, greased and
lined with greased baking
parchment
6–7-cm/2½–3-inch round
cookie cutter
piping bag, fitted with a star
nozzle/tip

makes 12

Preheat the oven to 180°C (350°F) Gas 4.

Prepare the Basic Vanilla Cake mixture as described on page 11, then transfer to the prepared baking pan and spread level with a palette knife. Bake on the middle shelf of the preheated oven for about 30 minutes or until a skewer inserted into the middle comes out clean. Let cool in the pan for 3–4 minutes, then turn out onto a wire rack to cool completely.

Wrap the cold cakes in clingfilm/plastic wrap and set aside until the following day.

The next day, when you are ready to assemble the cake, gently heat the strawberry jam to make it a little runnier, then strain it to get rid of any lumps.

Unwrap the cake and stamp out 12 circles using the cookie cutter. Brush the sides of each cake with a little of the jam.

Divide the Meringue Buttercream between 4 bowls and tint each one a different colour using the food colouring pastes. Using a palette knife, spread some meringue buttercream neatly around the side of each cake. Roll the sides in sugar strands/jimmies until evenly coated.

Spoon one colour of buttercream into the piping bag and pipe a lovely swirl on top of each cake. Repeat with the remaining buttercream and cakes. Press a gummy sweet/candy on the top of each cake just before serving.

With 3 layers of malted milk-flavoured cake, then a filling and covering of milk chocolate frosting, this is the cake equivalent of a huge bag of Maltesers or Whoppers.

malted chocolate cake

250 g/2 cups plain/all-purpose flour

2 teaspoons baking powder

½ teaspoon bicarbonate of/baking soda

a pinch of salt

150 g/10 tablespoons butter, soft

225 g/1 big cup (caster) sugar

3 large eggs, lightly beaten

1 teaspoon vanilla extract

175 ml/⅔ cup buttermilk

2 tablespoons malted milk powder

150 g/5 oz. milk chocolate-coated malted milk balls (Maltesers/Whoppers)

assorted chocolate sprinkles/nonpareils

malted chocolate frosting

200 g/6½ oz. dark/semisweet chocolate, finely chopped

150 g/5 oz. milk chocolate, finely chopped

250 ml/1 cup double/heavy cream

50 g/⅓ cup malted milk powder

2 tablespoons golden syrup

175 g/1½ sticks butter, soft

three 20-cm/8-inch round cake pans, greased and baselined with greased baking parchment

disposable piping bag

serves 10–12

Preheat the oven to 180°C (350°F) Gas 4.

Sift together the flour, baking powder, bicarbonate of/baking soda and salt.

Cream the butter and sugar in the bowl of a stand mixer until really pale and light – at least 3–4 minutes. Gradually add the beaten eggs to the creamed butter in 4 or 5 additions, mixing well between each addition and scraping down the bowl from time to time with a rubber spatula. Add the vanilla and mix to incorporate.

Gradually add the sifted dry ingredients to the cake mixture alternately with the buttermilk. Mix until smooth, the fold in the malted milk powder. Divide the mixture evenly between the prepared cake pans, scraping the mixture from the bowl using a rubber spatula. Spread level and bake on the middle shelf of the preheated oven for about 20 minutes or until a skewer inserted into the middle comes out clean. Let the cakes cool in the pans for 3–4 minutes, then turn out onto a wire rack to cool completely.

To make the malted chocolate frosting, tip the chopped chocolates into a medium heatproof bowl.

Put the cream, malted milk powder and syrup in a small, heavy-based saucepan over medium heat and whisk to combine. Stir occasionally until the cream just comes to the boil. Pour into the bowl of chocolate, stir and set aside to allow the chocolate to melt. Once melted, stir until silky smooth and leave until cold and starting to firm up. Gradually beat in the butter, one tablespoon at a time, until glossy and smooth.

Lightly crush about 100 g/3½ oz. of the milk chocolate-coated malted milk balls.

Place one of the cake layers on a serving dish and spread 3–4 tablespoons of the malted chocolate frosting over it, then scatter half the malted milk balls on top. Cover with a second cake layer. Repeat this process, finishing with the last cake layer. Spread all but 3 tablespoons of the remaining frosting evenly over the top and side of the cake using a palette knife. Spoon the reserved 3 tablespoons malted chocolate frosting into the piping bag and snip the end to a fine point. Pipe dots around the bottom edge of the cake and around the top edge too, if you like.

Arrange the whole malted milk balls and chocolate sprinkles/nonpareils on top of the cake just before serving.

The innocent-looking white frosting on this cake hides a spooky surprise underneath. The cake mixture is divided in two and tinted orange and green, then marbled together before baking. If you don't want to make the spider cupcakes you could always decorate the cake with spooky toy spiders and other ghoulish Halloween figures.

creepy halloween cake

1 quantity Basic Vanilla Cake (page 11)
orange food colouring paste
green food colouring paste
1 quantity Meringue Buttercream (page 16)
black food colouring paste
2 tablespoons black sprinkles/ nonpareils or sanding sugar
green and/or orange sanding sugar
250 g/2 cups royal icing sugar/mix
thin liquorice shoelaces
mini orange or yellow candy-coated chocolate drops

two 20-cm/8-inch round cake pans, greased and baselined with greased baking parchment

15-cm/6-inch round cake pan, greased and baselined with greased baking parchment

muffin pan, lined with 2–3 cupcake cases

disposable piping bag

serves 8–10

Preheat the oven to 180°C (350°F) Gas 4.

Prepare the Basic Vanilla Cake mixture as described on page 11. Divide the cake mixture between 2 bowls, and using the food colouring pastes, tint one bowl bright orange and the other bright green. Using a tablespoon, drop alternate spoonfuls of the 2 mixtures into the prepared cake pans, filling them halfway up. Fill the cupcake cases with alternate tablespoons of the cake mixtures, too. Tap the cake pans sharply on the work surface to level the mixture and drag a round-bladed knife through the 2 mixtures to create a marbled effect. Tap the cake pans on the work surface again. Repeat this process with the cupcakes in the muffin pan.

Bake everything on the middle shelves of the preheated oven for about 20–35 minutes, depending on their size, until a skewer inserted into the middle comes out clean. Let cool in the pans for 3–4 minutes, then turn out onto a wire rack to cool completely.

Tint 4 tablespoons of the Meringue Buttercream black using the food colouring paste.

To assemble the cake, place one of the larger cake layers on a serving dish and spread an even layer of the untinted buttercream over it. Top with the second, larger cake layer and gently press the cakes together. If the top cake has a domed surface, use a long serrated knife to trim off the dome and make it completely level. Spread a thin layer of untinted buttercream over the top and side of the cake, then refrigerate for 10 minutes. Cover the cake with another thin layer of untinted buttercream. Now repeat this process with the smaller cake layer.

Peel the cupcake cases off the cupcakes and slice the cupcakes in half horizontally. Cover them with the black buttercream and scatter with the black sprinkles/nonpareils or sanding sugar evenly over them to coat.

Place the smaller cake on top of the larger cake. Sprinkle green and/or orange sanding sugar over the cake.

Make up the royal icing as described on page 15 and tint black using the food colouring paste. Spoon the black icing into the piping bag and snip the end to a fine point. Pipe spider's webs all over the cake.

Press short lengths of the liquorice into the sides of the cupcakes as spider's legs and give each spider 2 orange or yellow eyes with the candy-coated chocolate drops. Arrange the spiders around the cake to serve.

1

2

3

Serve this especially pretty cake for afternoon tea or as a delicate dessert – it's particularly fitting for Mother's Day. The combination of lemon and raspberries is divine. Homemade lemon curd (see page 17) is utterly delicious and makes a difference, but if you're short of time look for a good storebought one.

lemon & raspberry roulade

75 g/½ cup plain/all-purpose flour, plus extra to dust

1½ teaspoons baking powder

75 g/¾ cup ground almonds

a pinch of salt

6 large eggs

175 g/1 scant cup (caster) sugar, plus extra to sprinkle

grated zest of 1 lemon

50 g/⅔ cup slivered almonds

juice from ½ lemon

6 tablespoons icing/confectioners' sugar

lemon & raspberry filling

350 ml/1½ cups double/heavy cream

150 g/⅔ cup mascarpone or crème fraîche

4 tablespoons good lemon curd (to make your own, see page 17)

300 g/1 pint raspberries, plus extra to serve

30 x 40-cm/12 x 16-inch Swiss-roll/jelly-roll pan, greased and lined with greased baking parchment

large piece of baking parchment

serves 8

Preheat the oven to 180°C (350°F) Gas 4. Dust the lined baking pan with flour and tip out any excess.

Sift together the flour, baking powder, ground almonds and salt.

Whisk the eggs and (caster) sugar in a stand mixer until pale, trebled in volume and the beaters leave a ribbon trail of mixture when lifted.

Fold in the dry ingredients and lemon zest using a large metal spoon. Gently pour the mixture into the prepared pan and spread level with a palette knife. Bake on the middle shelf of the preheated oven for about 12 minutes or until golden and just firm to the touch.

Sprinkle about 3 tablespoons (caster) sugar over the large sheet of baking parchment. Let the cake cool in the pan for 1 minute, then turn out onto the sugared baking parchment. Carefully peel off the baking paper, then roll up the cake, starting from a shorter end, with the clean paper inside the roll. (**1**)

Let cool completely while you make candied almonds. Tip the almonds and 1 tablespoon of the icing/confectioners' sugar into a small frying pan over

medium heat. Stir constantly until the sugar has dissolved and started to caramelize around the almonds. Tip onto baking parchment and let cool.

To make the lemon & raspberry filling, whip the cream and mascarpone until thickened and spreadable.

Unroll the roulade and spread the lemon curd over it, leaving a 2-cm/¾-inch border around the edges. Spread the whipped cream mixture over the lemon curd. (**2**)

Arrange the raspberries evenly over the roulade, then gently re-roll it, but this time use the sugared paper simply to help support the roll as you go – you don't want it to be inside the roulade. (**3**)

Place the roulade on a serving dish.

To make a lemon icing, beat together the lemon juice and 4–5 tablespoons icing/confectioners' sugar until smooth. Pour along the top of the roulade, allowing some to drizzle over the sides. Let set.

Scatter extra raspberries and the cooled candied almonds over the top. Dust the remaining icing/confectioners' sugar over the roulade to serve.

Brandied cherries, chocolate cake and lashings of whipped cream – sometimes the classic recipes are still popular for a good reason. You will need to prepare the brandied cherries at least a couple of days before you start to make this cake, so plan accordingly. They are so delicious, you'll find yourself eating some along the way, but don't get carried away! You'll need them to generously fill the cake. If you don't have the time or inclination to make them, you can use good morello cherries in syrup. This is the kind of cake that dads like – perhaps it's the combination of cream and booze – so it's perfect for a glamorous Father's Day dessert.

the ultimate black forest cake

100 g/⅔ cup dried sour cherries, roughly chopped

1 quantity Basic Chocolate Cake (see page 11, but follow the method on this page)

1 quantity Chocolate Ganache (page 14)

400 ml/1⅔ cups double/heavy cream

200 g/6½ oz. fresh cherries

brandied cherries

400-500 g/about 1 lb. fresh cherries

200 ml/¾ cup brandy

100 g/½ cup (caster) sugar

large, clean, screw-top jar

three 20-cm/8-inch round cake pans, greased and baselined with greased baking parchment

2 piping bags, fitted with star nozzles/tips

serves 10

Make the brandied cherries 3–4 days in advance. Pit the cherries and place in the screw-top jar. Add the brandy and sugar, cover tightly with the lid and give the jar a vigorous shake to dissolve the sugar. Set aside for 3–4 days, shaking the jar occasionally.

When you are ready to bake the cake, preheat the oven to 180°C (350°F) Gas 4.

Put the chopped sour cherries in a small saucepan with 2–3 tablespoons of the macerated cherry liqueur from the jar of brandied cherries. Set over low heat and gently warm for a couple of minutes so that the cherries plump up and absorb almost all the liqueur. Remove from the heat and let cool.

Prepare the Basic Chocolate Cake mixture as described on page 11, then fold in the plumped dried cherries and any remaining liqueur in the pan. Divide the mixture evenly between the prepared cake pans, scraping the mixture from the bowl using a rubber spatula. Spread level and bake on the middle shelf of the preheated oven for about 25–30 minutes or until a skewer inserted into the middle comes out clean.

Let the cakes cool in the pans for 3–4 minutes, then turn out onto a wire rack to cool completely.

Put the Chocolate Ganache in a bowl with 1 tablespoon of the macerated cherry liqueur from the jar and stir gently. Set aside to thicken to spreading consistency. Set aside 3 tablespoons of the cherry ganache to decorate the top of the cake.

Drain the brandied cherries from the jar, reserving the liqueur for use another time. Halve the drained cherries and set aside.

Whip the cream until it will stand in floppy peaks.

Place one of the cake layers on a serving dish and spread half the cherry ganache over it. Scatter the brandied cherries, then cover with about one-third of the whipped cream. Cover with a second cake layer. Repeat this process, finishing with the last cake layer. Gently press the cakes together. Using a palette knife, spread most of the remaining whipped cream over the top of the cake. Fill the piping bags separately with the remaining whipped cream and reserved 3 tablespoons cherry ganache. Pipe swirls of cream and ganache rosettes on top of the cake and decorate with the fresh cherries.

I love using fancy-shaped cake pans; it's an easy way to elevate a simple cake to the realms of something quite special. This is one of my favourite cakes – it keeps really well, can be made in advance and is sure to please adults and children alike. I have decorated it simply with wafer flowers, available at sugarcraft suppliers or online (see page 128), but I love to use fresh orange blossoms when they are in season and crystallize them (see page 78). Which lovely mum wouldn't love to be made this beautiful cake on Mother's Day?

orange blossom & almond cake

225 g/15 tablespoons butter, soft, plus extra to grease

150 g/1 cup plus 3 tablespoons plain/all-purpose flour, plus extra to dust

200 g/2 cups ground almonds

2 teaspoons baking powder

a pinch of salt

275 g/1⅓ cups (caster) sugar

4 large eggs, lightly beaten

grated zest of 2 oranges and juice of 1 juice of 1 lemon

2 teaspoons orange blossom water

wafer flowers, to decorate (see page 128)

orange glaze

finely grated zest and juice from 1 orange

1 tablespoon Grand Marnier or Cointreau (optional)

125 g/1 cup icing/confectioners' sugar

2 tablespoons apricot jam

2-litre/quart tube, bundt or kugelhopf pan

serves 8

Preheat the oven to 170°C (325°F) Gas 3.

Melt a little of the extra butter and brush it inside the cake pan, making sure that the pan is thoroughly and evenly coated. Dust the pan with flour and tip out any excess.

Sift together the flour, ground almonds, baking powder and salt.

Cream the butter and sugar in the bowl of a stand mixer until really pale and light – at least 3–4 minutes. Gradually add the beaten eggs to the creamed butter in 4 or 5 additions, mixing well between each addition and scraping down the bowl from time to time with a rubber spatula.

Add the orange zest and juice, lemon juice and orange blossom water. Tip the sifted dry ingredients into the bowl and beat for another 30–40 seconds to thoroughly combine. Spoon the mixture into the prepared cake pan, spread level and bake just below the middle shelf of the preheated oven for about 40–45 minutes until golden brown, well risen and a wooden skewer inserted into the middle comes out clean. Leave the oven on.

Let cool in the pan for no more than 2 minutes, then carefully turn out onto a wire rack and let cool for 30 minutes.

To make the orange glaze, bring the orange zest and juice and Grand Marnier, if using, to the boil in a small saucepan, then simmer for 1 minute to reduce slightly. Remove from the heat, add the icing/confectioners' sugar and stir to dissolve. Let cool and thicken slightly.

Gently heat the apricot jam to make it a little runnier, then strain it to get rid of any lumps.

Brush the jam over the still-warm cake, covering it completely, and let set for 5 minutes. Now brush some of the glaze over the cake, leave for 5 minutes, then brush again with the remaining glaze. Leave for another 5 minutes, then slide the cake onto a baking sheet and put back in the oven. Turn off the heat and leave for 5 minutes to allow the glaze to become translucent.

Remove the cake from the oven and let cool completely. Decorate with wafer flowers just before serving.

This cake is bettered by being made at least 24 hours before you want to serve it – the spices become mellow and the cake becomes stickier. The candied pineapple slices are delicious eaten on their own, but they transform this cake from an everyday teatime treat to a Father's Day show-stopper!

rum & ginger spiced cake with candied pineapple

150 g/10 tablespoons butter

75 g/⅓ cup golden syrup/light corn syrup

75 g/⅓ cup dark treacle/molasses

175 g/¾ cup plus 2 tablespoons dark muscovado sugar

4 nuggets of stem ginger in syrup, finely chopped

3 tablespoons dark rum

½ teaspoon bicarbonate of/ baking soda

200 g/1⅔ cups plain/all-purpose flour

1 teaspoon baking powder

3 teaspoons ground ginger

1 big teaspoon ground cinnamon

¼ teaspoon ground allspice

¼ teaspoon grated nutmeg

a pinch of salt

3 medium eggs, lightly beaten

½ medium, ripe pineapple

½ quantity Cream Cheese Frosting (page 14)

rum & ginger syrup

100 g/½ cup (caster) sugar

juice of 1 lime

4 cm/1½ inches fresh ginger, peeled and roughly chopped

3 tablespoons dark rum

1 cinnamon stick

2-lb. loaf pan (26 x 11 cm/9 x 5 inches), greased and lined with a strip of greased baking parchment

baking sheet, lined with nonstick baking parchment

serves 8

Preheat the oven to 170°C (325°F) Gas 3.

First make the rum & ginger syrup. Put all the ingredients along with 3 tablespoons water in a small saucepan over medium heat. Bring to the boil, stirring to dissolve the sugar, then simmer for 3–4 minutes until slightly thickened. Remove from the heat and let cool to allow the ginger and cinnamon to infuse the syrup.

Put the butter, syrup, treacle/molasses and sugar in a small pan and heat gently to dissolve the sugar and melt the butter. Add half the chopped ginger, rum and 100 ml/6 tablespoons boiling water and mix to combine. Stir in the bicarbonate of/baking soda – beware, the mixture will foam – and set aside.

Sift the flour, baking powder, spices and salt into a large mixing bowl and make a well in the middle. Add the eggs and butter-syrup mixture in 3 batches, beating well after each addition. Stir until silky smooth, then transfer to the prepared loaf pan. Tap the pan on the work surface to release any large air bubbles and bake just below the middle of the preheated oven for about 45–50 minutes or until a skewer inserted into the middle of the cake comes out clean. Turn the oven down to 110°C (225°F) Gas ¼.

Let cool in the pan for 3–4 minutes while you strain the rum & ginger syrup. Prick the hot cake all over with a wooden skewer and slowly drizzle 1–2 tablespoons of the syrup over the top, allowing it to soak in. Let cool in the pan.

Peel the pineapple and cut it in half lengthwise through the core. Using a long, sharp knife or mandoline, cut the pineapple into wafer-thin slices and arrange on the prepared baking sheet. Brush each slice with the rum & ginger syrup and bake on the middle shelf of the oven for about 1 hour until slightly golden and crisp. You will need to turn the slices over after halfway through cooking and turn the baking sheet around in the oven to ensure that the slices dry evenly. Lay the slices on a wire rack and let cool until cold and crisp.

Stir the remaining chopped ginger into the Cream Cheese Frosting. Place the cake on a serving dish, cover the top with frosting and arrange the candied pineapple slices on top just before serving.

1 quantity Basic Vanilla Cake (page 11,
but follow the method on this page)
1 tablespoon chopped freeze-dried
strawberries
50 g/½ cup ground almonds
½ teaspoon rosewater
1 teaspoon grated lemon zest
4 tablespoons strawberry jam
1 quantity Meringue Buttercream
(page 16)
500 g/1 lb. fresh strawberries

crystallized flowers
fresh flowers (non-toxic, unsprayed
and untreated)
1 egg white
200 g/1 cup (caster) sugar
*three 20-cm/8-inch round cake pans,
greased and baselined with greased
baking parchment*

serves 10–12

This is a cake for high summer when the roses are in full bloom and the strawberries are at their sweetest.
It would suit a hen/bachelorette, or a new mum. You will need to make the crystallized roses at least
2 hours before you plan to serve the cake, and be sure to use non-toxic and unsprayed flowers.

rose & strawberry cake
with crystallized roses

To make the crystallized flowers, carefully remove the
petals from the fresh flowers. Keep small buds whole. (**1**)

Lightly beat the egg white with a fork for 5 seconds,
then, taking one petal at a time and using a soft brush,
lightly coat both sides of the petal with egg white.
Sprinkle sugar over both sides of the petal to completely
cover. (**2**)

Let dry in a single layer on a wire rack. Petals will dry
and harden in about 2–4 hours and are best used within
48 hours of making, as their colour will start to fade. (**3**)

When you are ready to make the cake, preheat the oven
to 180°C (350°F) Gas 4.

Prepare the Basic Vanilla Cake mixture as described
on page 11, adding the freeze-dried strawberries,
ground almonds, rosewater and lemon zest to the
mixture with the final addition of flour. Mix until thoroughly
incorporated, then divide evenly between the prepared
pans and spread level with a palette knife. Bake the

cakes on the middle shelf of the preheated oven for
about 25 minutes or until a skewer inserted into the
middle comes out clean. Let the cakes cool in the
pans for 3–4 minutes, then turn out onto a wire rack
to cool completely.

Gently heat the strawberry jam to make it a little runnier,
then strain it to get rid of any lumps. Fold the jam into
the Meringue Buttercream.

Take three-quarters of the strawberries, hull and slice
them. Reserve the remaining strawberries for decoration.

Place one of the cake layers on a serving dish and
spread one-third of the meringue buttercream over it.
Scatter half the sliced strawberries over it, then cover
with another cake layer. Repeat this process.

Place the third cake layer on top and very gently press
the layers together. Cover the top of the cake with the
remaining meringue buttercream and decorate with the
crystallized roses and reserved whole strawberries.

You will need to bake the cake layers for these little cakes one day before you plan to decorate them. They will be much easier to cut into neat squares the day after baking. Dried lavender is now available from some supermarkets and sugarcraft suppliers, but if you use your own, make sure it is unsprayed and uncoloured. Serve these little cakes at a sophisticated afternoon tea – Mother's Day would be a perfect occasion.

lilac & lavender petits fours

150 g/1 cup plus 3 tablespoons plain/all-purpose flour

25 g/¼ cup ground almonds

2 teaspoons baking powder

½ teaspoon bicarbonate of/baking soda

a pinch of salt

175 g/¾ cup (caster) sugar

2 teaspoons dried lavender flowers

175 g/1½ sticks butter, soft

3 large eggs, lightly beaten

grated zest of ½ lemon

3 tablespoons sour cream, room temperature

4–5 tablespoons apricot jam

4 tablespoons good lemon curd (to make your own, see page 17)

icing/confectioners' sugar, to dust

500 g/1 lb. ready-to-roll royal icing

lilac food colouring paste

½ quantity Royal Icing (page 15)

green food colouring paste

two 20-cm/8-inch square cake pans, greased and baselined with baking parchment

2 disposable piping bags

ribbons

makes 9

Start making the cake the day before you want to serve it. Preheat the oven to 180°C (350°F) Gas 4.

Sift together the flour, ground almonds, baking powder, bicarbonate of/baking soda and salt.

Whizz the (caster) sugar and lavender in a food processor for 10 seconds. This will bring out the lovely lavender fragrance.

Cream the butter and lavender sugar in the bowl of a stand mixer until really pale and light – at least 3–4 minutes. Gradually add the beaten eggs to the creamed butter in 4 or 5 additions, mixing well between each addition and scraping down the bowl from time to time with a rubber spatula. Add the lemon zest. Add the sifted dry ingredients and sour cream and mix until smooth. Divide the mixture evenly between the prepared cake pans, scraping the mixture from the bowl using a rubber spatula. Spread level and bake on the middle shelf of the preheated oven for about 20 minutes or until a skewer inserted into the middle comes out clean. Let cool in the pans for 3–4 minutes, then turn out onto a wire rack to cool completely.

Wrap the cold cakes in clingfilm/plastic wrap and set aside until the following day.

The next day, when you are ready to assemble the cake, gently heat the apricot jam to make it a little runnier, then strain it to get rid of any lumps.

Place one of the cake layers on a work surface and spread the lemon curd over it, then cover with the other cake. Gently press the cakes together. Trim the edges if they need neatening, then cut into 9 even cubes. Brush the top and sides of each cube with the jam.

Dust a work surface with icing/confectioners' sugar. Tint the ready-to-roll royal icing a delicate shade of lilac using the food colouring paste. Divide it into 9 even pieces and roll each one out into a square roughly 2 mm/¹⁄₁₆ inch thick. Cover each cake cube with a square of the icing, using your hands to smooth the top and sides. Trim off any excess icing and let the cakes dry on a board.

Divide the Royal Icing between 2 bowls. Tint one bowl green and the other lavender purple using the food colouring pastes. Spoon the green icing into a piping bag, snip the end to a fine point and pipe 3 stalks and 2 leaves for the lavender on top of each cake. Use the purple icing to pipe the lavender flowers on each stalk.

Let the icing dry completely before tying a pretty ribbon around the bottom edge of each cake.

Here's a beautiful cake that's all wrapped up like a gift box. It will feed a large crowd and would be ideal for a small wedding.

ribbons & bows cake

2 quantities Basic Vanilla Cake (page 11)
200 g/6½ oz. white gum paste
red food colouring paste
icing/confectioners' sugar, to dust
1 quantity Meringue Buttercream (page 16)
6 tablespoons good jam or lemon curd (to make your own lemon curd, see page 17)
1 kg/2 lbs. ready-to-roll royal icing
green food colouring paste

two 23-cm/9-inch round cake pans, greased and baselined with greased baking parchment
two 18-cm/7-inch round cake pans, greased and baselined with greased baking parchment
dowel rods and shears

serves about 20

Preheat the oven to 180°C (350°F) Gas 4.

Prepare the first quantity of Basic Vanilla Cake mixture as described on page 11, then divide evenly between the 2 larger cake pans, scraping the mixture from the bowl using a rubber spatula. Spread level and bake on the middle shelf of the preheated oven for about 25 minutes or until a skewer inserted into the middle comes out clean. Let the cakes cool in the pans for 3–4 minutes, then turn out onto a wire rack to cool completely. Leave the oven on. Wash and dry one of the larger cake pans, grease it and baseline it with greased baking parchment again. Prepare the second quantity of Basic Vanilla Cake mixture, divide evenly between the re-prepared larger cake pan and the two smaller cake pans and bake for 20–25 minutes. Let cool as above.

Tint the gum paste pink using the food colouring paste. Break off a small amount of paste at a time to work with and keep the remainder tightly covered in clingfilm/plastic wrap. Very lightly dust a work surface with icing/confectioners' sugar and roll the paste out to a thickness of 1–2 mm/¹⁄₁₆ inch. Cut the paste into 8 strips about 2–3 cm/1 inch wide and 10 cm/4 inches long. Lightly brush one end of each strip with a little cold water, fold the strip over to make a loop and pinch together to seal – this will form one side of a bow. Repeat to make 8 loops. Pinch 2 loops together to make a bow. Repeat with the remaining loops to make 4 bows. Cut 4 strips of gum paste 1 cm/⅜ inch wide and roughly 3 cm/1¼ inches long and wrap this around the join in the middle of each bow. Seal with a dab of cold water, then let dry. Roll out more gum paste and cut into 8 strips roughly 2–3 cm/1 inch wide and 4 cm/1½ inches long. Snip a triangle out of one end of each strip to look like ribbons. Make 16–20 smaller bows as above – these do not need matching ribbons.

To assemble the cakes, lay one of the larger cake layers on a serving dish. Spread 3 tablespoons of the Meringue Buttercream over the top, then 2 tablespoons of the jam. Top with another cake layer and repeat this process until you have a stack of 3 larger cake layers. Cover the top and side of the cake with a smooth layer of buttercream. Loosely cover the cake with clingfilm/plastic wrap and refrigerate until the buttercream is firm. Repeat this process with the smaller cake layers.

Break off 100 g/3½ oz. of the ready-to-roll royal icing and tint green using the food colouring paste, then cover until needed. Colour another 100 g/3½ oz. of icing the same shade of pink as the gum-paste bows and cover until needed. Tint the remaining icing a paler shade of green. Lightly dust a work surface with icing/confectioners' sugar and roll out two-thirds of the pale green icing. Use this to cover the top and side of the larger cake, smoothing it over with your hands. Trim off any excess icing at the base of the cake. Use the remaining pale green icing to cover the smaller cake.

Make a note of the circumference of each cake. Roll the darker green icing out until 1–2 mm/¹⁄₁₆ inch thick and cut into 2 strips about 2 cm/¾ inch wide and the length of each cake circumference. Lightly brush the bottom edge of each cake with water and secure the green icing strip. Repeat this with the pink icing, making the strips thinner and securing them along the darker green strips on the cake. Make 4 extra pink strips and secure across the top of the cakes in a cross shape.

Stack the cakes on top of one another using dowel rods as support (see page 100 for instructions). Secure the gum-paste bows on top and around each cake using a tiny dab of cold water.

175 g/6 oz. undyed glacé cherries
225 g/8 oz. natural marzipan
275 g/2 cups plus 2 tablespoons self-raising flour
1 teaspoon baking powder
½ teaspoon ground cinnamon
a pinch of salt
75 g/¾ cup ground almonds
200 g/13 tablespoons butter, soft
200 g/1 cup (caster) sugar
4 large eggs, lightly beaten
1 teaspoon vanilla extract
finely grated zest of 1 lemon
2 tablespoons milk
3 tablespoons apricot or cherry jam
icing/confectioners' sugar, to dust
225 g/8 oz. ready-to-roll royal icing

cherry blossoms
100 g/3½ oz. white gum paste
red food colouring paste
pink lustre dust
2 tablespoons Royal Icing (page 15)
pink sugar sprinkles/nonpareils
assorted flower-shaped cutters
disposable piping bag
*20-cm/8-inch springform cake pan, greased
and lined with greased baking parchment*

serves 8–10

This is a delicious, old-fashioned kind of cake that has been made more special with the marzipan hidden inside it which melts into the mixture when baking, and the adornment of gum-paste cherry blossoms. Decorate it with crystallized cherries and bay leaves if you prefer.

cherry & almond cake

Make the cherry blossoms at least 24 hours before you plan to serve the cake.

Tint the gum paste pink using the food colouring paste. You can tint portions of the paste in different shades of pink (or leave white) if you like. Lightly dust the work surface with icing/confectioners' sugar and roll the gum paste out no thicker than 2 mm/1⁄16 inch. Using the flower cutters, stamp out shapes and curl and crimp the edges with your fingers. Arrange the blossoms on crumpled baking parchment. Using a small brush, lightly dust pink lustre dust on the edges of each blossom. Let dry overnight.

The next day, tint the Royal Icing pink and spoon into the piping bag. Snip the end into a fine point and pipe a dot of pink icing in the middle of each blossom. Cover the dots with sugar sprinkles/nonpareils and let dry.

When you are ready to bake the cake, preheat the oven to 170°C (325°F) Gas 3.

Rinse the glacé cherries under warm water, thoroughly pat dry on kitchen paper/paper towels, cut in half and tip into a large bowl.

Roll 75 g/2½ oz. of the marzipan between 2 sheets of baking parchment and cut into an 18-cm/7-inch disc.

Sift together the flour, baking powder, cinnamon and salt and add the ground almonds.

Cream the butter and (caster) sugar in the bowl of a stand mixer until really pale and light – at least 3–4 minutes. Gradually add the beaten eggs to the creamed butter in 4 or 5 additions, mixing well between each addition and scraping down the bowl from time to time with a rubber spatula. Add the vanilla and lemon zest. Add the sifted dry ingredients and milk and beat again for 20 seconds. Fold in the cherries.

Spoon two-thirds of the cake mixture into the prepared cake pan, spread level with a palette knife and lay the marzipan disc on top. Spoon the remaining mixture into the pan and spread level. Bake just below the middle shelf of the preheated oven for about 55 minutes or until golden, well risen and a skewer inserted in the middle comes out with a moist crumb.

Let cool in the pan for 10–15 minutes, then carefully turn out onto a wire rack and let cool completely before icing.

Gently heat the jam to make it a little runnier, then strain it to get rid of any lumps.

Lightly dust the work surface with icing/confectioners' sugar and roll the remaining marzipan out into a neat disc the same size as the top of the cake – use the cake pan as a guide. Brush some jam over the cake and lay the marzipan on top. Lightly brush again with jam.

Roll the fondant icing out to the same size as the top of the cake and carefully and neatly cover the marzipan. Trim the edges if necessary to create a perfectly neat edge.

Pipe a small dot of royal icing beneath each cherry blossom and arrange on top of the cake.

8 tablespoons raspberry jam
2 quantities Chocolate Ganache (page 14)
about 40 storebought macarons

middle layer
6 large eggs
300 g/10 oz. dark/bittersweet chocolate
75 g/5 tablespoons butter
250 g/1¼ cups (caster) sugar
a pinch of salt
150 g/1½ cup ground almonds
1 tablespoon chopped freeze-dried raspberries

top & bottom layers
12 large eggs
600 g/20 oz. dark/bittersweet chocolate
150 g/10 tablespoons butter
500 g/2½ cups (caster) sugar
a pinch of salt
300 g/3 cups ground almonds
2 tablespoons chopped freeze-dried raspberries

25-cm/10-inch; 18-cm/7-inch; and 10-cm/4-inch round cake pans

large cake stand; 18-cm/7-inch and 10-cm/4-inch cake boards

serves 30–40

The cakes for this monumental chocolate confection can be made a good 3 days in advance, as they will come to no harm if they are well wrapped once completely cold. Buy the French macarons from a fancy bakery where they make them in just about every colour under the sun and serve this stunning cake at an elegant wedding.

macaron wedding cake

Grease and line the cake pans with a double thickness of greased baking parchment. Wrap the outside of the largest pan in a double thickness of baking parchment and secure with kitchen twine.

Preheat the oven to 170°C (325°F) Gas 3.

To make the middle layer of cake, take 5 of the eggs and separate the yolks and whites. Leave the remaining egg whole. Roughly chop the chocolate and butter and put in a heatproof bowl set over a pan of barely simmering water. Do not let the base of the bowl touch the water. Stir until smooth and thoroughly combined. Remove from the heat and cool slightly.

Put the egg yolks, whole egg and sugar in the bowl of a stand mixer and whisk on medium–high speed until the mixture has doubled in volume, is thick, pale and very light and will leave a ribbon trail when the whisk is lifted from the bowl. Mix in the cooled, melted chocolate and butter and stir until smooth.

Whisk the egg whites and salt in a large, clean bowl until they just hold a stiff peak. Using a large metal spoon, fold the ground almonds and freeze-dried raspberries into the mixture, followed by one-third of the egg whites. Carefully fold in the remaining egg whites and then pour the mixture into the prepared 18-cm/7-inch cake pan, spread level and bake in the bottom third of the oven for about 1 hour 20 minutes or until a skewer inserted in the middle comes out with a moist crumb. Let the cake cool in the pan for 30 minutes, then turn out onto a wire rack to cool completely. Leave the oven on.

Now follow the instructions above again but use the ingredients for the top and bottom layers of the cake. Take 10 of the eggs and separate the yolks and whites. Leave the remaining 2 eggs whole. Make the cake mixture as described, then divide between the 25-cm/10-inch and 10-cm/4-inch cake pans. Bake for about 1 hour 30 minutes for the larger cake and 35 minutes for the smaller cake.

When the cakes are completely cold, wrap in clingfilm/plastic wrap until you are ready to frost and assemble them.

When you are ready to assemble the cakes, gently heat the jam to make it a little runnier, then strain it to get rid of any lumps.

Place the largest cake on the cake stand and each of the other cakes on their matching cake boards. Brush the jam over the tops and sides of all 3 cakes.

Using a palette knife, spread the Chocolate Ganache smoothly over the tops and sides of each cake and let set in a cool place for about 30 minutes.

Just before serving, stack the cakes one on top of the other. Apply a small blob of ganache on one side of each macaron and position around the edges of the cakes. Top the cake with a couple more macarons, if you like.

Croquembouche means 'crunch in the mouth'. Here is my simplified but by no means less impressive version of this classic French wedding cake. Bite-size choux buns are filled with either vanilla or chocolate crème pâtissière, dipped in amber-coloured caramel and assembled in a pyramid-shaped tower. Finally, the whole gâteau is then decorated with gold and silver dragées and candied rose petals and encased in feather-light spun sugar.

croquembouche

400 g/2 cups (caster) sugar
gold and silver dragées
candied rose petals

choux pastry
200 g/1²⁄₃ cups plain/all-purpose flour
2 teaspoons (caster) sugar
a pinch of salt
125 ml/½ cup milk
125 ml/½ cup water
110 g/7 tablespoons butter, diced
7 medium eggs, lightly beaten

crème filling – you will need to make TWICE this quantity
6 medium egg yolks
75 g/⅓ cup (caster) sugar
3 tablespoons plain/all-purpose flour
1 tablespoon cornflour/cornstarch
a pinch of salt
500 ml/2 cups milk
1 teaspoon vanilla extract

to finish the crème filling – only ONE quantity needed
75 g/2½ oz. dark/bittersweet chocolate, finely chopped
300 ml/1¼ cups double/heavy cream

3 piping bags, a plain 1-cm/³⁄₈-inch nozzle/tip and 2 small plain nozzle/tips

2 or 3 baking sheets, lined with baking parchment

serves 20

To make the choux pastry, preheat the oven to 220°C (425°F) Gas 7.

Sift together the flour, sugar and salt and set aside.

Pour the milk and water into a medium saucepan. Add the diced butter and heat, without boiling, until the butter has melted. Bring to a fast boil and immediately remove from the heat. Working quickly, tip the sifted dry ingredients into the pan and beat furiously with a wooden spoon until smooth and the mixture comes away from the side of the pan.

Let cool slightly, then gradually add the beaten eggs, mixing well between each addition, until the mixture will reluctantly drop from the spoon. You may not need to add all of the egg.

Spoon the choux pastry into a piping bag fitted with the 1-cm/³⁄₈-inch nozzle/tip. Now turn to the instructions overleaf to make the choux buns.

While the freshly baked choux buns are cooling, make the vanilla and chocolate crèmes.

To make the first batch of crème filling, in a medium, heatproof bowl, whisk together the egg yolks and (caster) sugar until pale and light. Add the flour, cornflour/cornstarch and salt. Pour the milk into a heavy-based saucepan, add the vanilla and heat until it is only just boiling. Pour this over the egg mixture, whisking constantly with a balloon whisk until smooth. Return the mixture to the pan and heat gently until just boiling and thickened. Taste a little of the crème – you should not be able to taste the flour. If you can still taste flour, continue to cook for another 30 seconds.

Strain the crème through a fine sieve/strainer into a clean bowl, cover the surface with clingfilm/plastic wrap and let cool completely.

Make the second batch of crème filling following the method above. To finish, add the chopped chocolate to the strained crème at the end. Stir until smooth, cover the surface with clingfilm/plastic wrap and let cool completely.

Once both of the crèmes are cold, whip the double/heavy cream until firm and fold half into the cooled vanilla crème and half into the chocolate crème. Refrigerate until needed.

Now turn to the instructions overleaf to fill the choux buns.

Pipe even mounds of choux pastry no larger than the size of a walnut on one prepared baking sheet. Leave some space between each one. (**1**)

Bake this first batch on the middle shelf of the preheated oven for about 15 minutes or until golden brown and puffed up to double the size. Leave the oven on. Meanwhile, pipe a second batch and bake when the first batch has come out of the oven. Repeat until all the pastry has been used up – you should make roughly 50 buns. Let cool completely.

Make a small hole on the underside of each choux bun using a wooden skewer. Spoon the vanilla crème into a piping bag fitted with a small plain nozzle/tip and fill half of the choux buns through the hole you've just made. Repeat with the chocolate crème and the remaining buns. (**2**)

To make caramel, half-fill the kitchen sink with cold water, ready for later. Put the 400 g/2 cups sugar and 1 tablespoon water in a small, heavy-based saucepan over low heat. Cook to completely dissolve the sugar. Bring to the boil and cook until it turns to an amber-coloured caramel.

Remove from the heat and plunge the bottom of the pan into the sink of cold water. Using tongs, pick up one choux bun and dip the top into the caramel, allowing the excess to drip back into the pan. Place the bun back on its baking sheet. (**3**)

Repeat for all of the choux buns. If the caramel starts to harden in the pan, return to a low heat for 30 seconds to re-melt.

(4) Once all the buns have been dipped in caramel, stack them up in a pyramid on a serving dish. Arrange the dragées and candied rose petals around the choux.

Re-melt the last of the caramel in the pan by putting over low heat again. Using 2 forks or spoons, pull the caramel from the pan in long, fine strands and twirl the spun sugar around the croquembouche. Serve!

For sheer wow-factor, this has to be my favourite cake in this collection. Homemade ladyfingers (also known as savoiardi biscuits or sponge fingers) are easy as pie to make and they're a taste revelation! Not only that, but they also keep very well in an airtight container, meaning that you can make them well in advance. A word of warning: this is the kind of cake creation which demands patience, precision and devotion! But the rewards (and ensuing compliments) make it all worth while...

white chocolate & summer berry
charlotte cake

charlotte cake – you will need to make TWICE this quantity

200 g/1⅔ cups plain/all-purpose flour, plus extra to dust

2 teaspoons baking powder

a pinch of salt

50 g/3½ tablespoons butter

175 g/6 oz. white chocolate, chopped

75 ml/⅓ cup milk

5 large eggs

175 g/¾ cup plus 2 tablespoons (caster) sugar

1 teaspoon vanilla extract or seeds from ½ vanilla pod/bean

25-cm/10-inch; 18-cm/7-inch; and 10-cm/4-inch cake pans, greased and baselined with greased baking parchment

serves 30–40

Preheat the oven to 180°C (350°F) Gas 4.

Dust all 3 of the cake pans with flour, tap on the work surface and tip out any excess.

To make the first batch of charlotte cake, sift the flour, baking powder and salt onto a sheet of baking parchment.

Put the butter, chocolate and milk in a small, heavy-based saucepan over low heat. Heat, stirring, until the butter and chocolate have completely melted. Remove from the heat and let cool slightly.

Put the eggs, sugar and vanilla in the bowl of a stand mixer and whisk on medium–high speed until the mixture has trebled in volume, is thick, pale, very light and will leave a ribbon trail when the whisk is lifted from the bowl.

Using a large metal spoon, gently fold the sifted dry ingredients into the egg mixture. Pour the melted chocolate mixture around the inside edge of the bowl and gently fold in.

Divide the mixture between the prepared cake pans, filling each pan to the same depth. Bake on the middle shelf of the preheated oven for 10–12 minutes for the small pan, 15–17 minutes for the medium pan and 30 minutes for the large pan. The cakes should be golden, well risen and a skewer inserted in the middle should come out clean. Let cool in the pans for a couple of minutes before turning out onto a wire rack to cool completely. Leave the oven on.

Wash and dry all the cake pans, grease and baseline with greased baking parchment again. Dust the pans with flour, tap on the work surface and tip out any excess.

Make the second batch of charlotte cake, following the method above.

Now see overleaf for instructions on making the ladyfingers and the frosting, and assembling the cake.

ladyfingers

4 large eggs, separated

1 teaspoon vanilla extract

150 g/¾ cup caster/superfine
sugar, plus extra to sprinkle

a pinch of salt

75 g/⅔ cup plain/all-purpose
flour

red food colouring paste

*3 baking sheets, lined with
nonstick baking parchment*

*2 large piping bags, fitted with
1-cm/⅜-inch plain nozzles/tips*

makes about 60 ladyfingers

To make the ladyfingers, preheat the oven to 180°C (350°F) Gas 4.

On one sheet of the nonstick baking parchment, draw 2 pairs of parallel lines 7–8 cm/3 inches apart. Flip the paper over – you should be able to see the marks through the paper. Repeat with the 2 remaining sheets of paper.

Put the egg yolks, vanilla and half the sugar in the bowl of a stand mixer. Whisk on high speed until thick, pale and the mixture will leave a ribbon trail when the whisk is lifted from the bowl.

In another bowl, whisk the egg whites and salt until stiff but not dry. Gradually add the remaining sugar and whisk. Fold the egg whites into the yolk mixture using a large metal spoon or rubber spatula. Sift the flour over the mixture and fold in.

Spoon half the mixture into another bowl. Tint pink using the food colouring paste – add the paste slowly using a cocktail stick/toothpick or wooden skewer and gently stir in until the mixture is evenly coloured. You will need to make the mixture a stronger colour than you imagine.

Spoon the pink mixture into one of the piping bags. Pipe even-sized ladyfingers onto the sheets of baking parchment, using the lines as a guide and keeping the ladyfingers at least 2 cm/¾ inch apart. Sprinkle extra sugar over them and set aside for 5 minutes.

Meanwhile, repeat with the untinted mixture in the other piping bag.

Bake the ladyfingers in batches on the middle shelf of the preheated oven for about 10 minutes or until crisp and pale golden brown.

Let cool on the baking sheets.

Now see overleaf for instructions on how to make the frosting and assemble the cake.

To make a summer berry purée for the buttercream, tip the fruit, sugar, lemon juice and the halved vanilla pod/bean into a saucepan over low–medium heat. Cook until thickened and slightly jammy. Push the fruit through a nylon sieve/strainer and set aside until cold.

Fold the cooled summer berry purée into the Meringue Buttercream until thoroughly combined.

To assemble the cake, brush some of the Rum or Brandy Syrup over one of the large cake layers. Spread 4 tablespoons of the berry buttercream over the top and cover with the second, large cake layer. Brush more rum syrup over the top. Using a palette knife, spread an even layer of buttercream over the top and sides of the cake. Transfer carefully to the cake stand.

Repeat this process with the medium cake layers on the 18-cm/7-inch cake board, and the small cake layers on the 10-cm/4-inch cake board.

Insert one piece of dowel rod into the large cake and make a note of the height of the cake. Remove the rod and, using shears, cut 7 pieces of dowel slightly longer than the height of the cake. Repeat this process for the medium cake but using 5 pieces of dowel.

Insert 6 pieces of the dowel into the larger cake in a 16-cm/6½-inch circle so that they will support the medium cake. Insert the seventh piece in the very middle of the cake. Repeat this process for the medium cake using 4 dowel rods in a 12-cm/5-inch circle, and the fifth in the very middle of the cake.

Place the medium cake carefully on the large cake, resting it on the bottom row of dowel rods. Place the small cake on the medium cake, resting it on the top of the dowel rods. Arrange the ladyfingers in alternate colours around the outside of each cake. Scatter more whole berries around the top edges of each cake. Tie pink ribbons around each cake and serve.

to assemble

250 g/1 pint strawberries,
hulled and halved

200 g/1½ cups raspberries

150 g/1 generous cup redcurrants

75 g/⅓ cup (caster) sugar

juice of ½ lemon

½ vanilla pod/bean

2 quantities Meringue
Buttercream (page 16)

1 quantity Rum or Brandy Syrup
(page 17)

extra whole berries, to decorate

*large cake stand; 18-cm/7-inch
and 10-cm/4-inch cake boards*

dowel rods and shears

pink ribbons

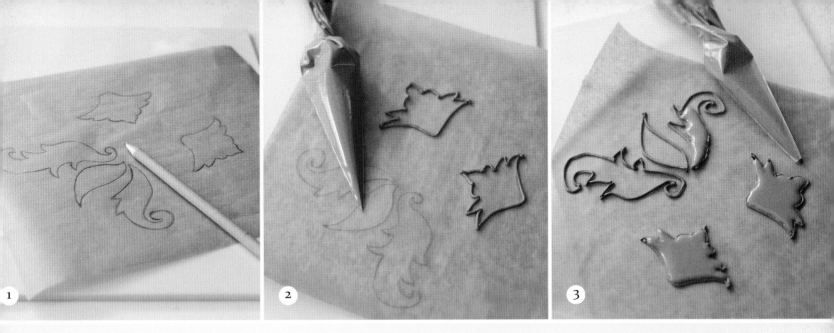

If you are not confident in piping patterns and shapes directly onto a cake, you might find this method of decoration much simpler. Keep the design simple and make the shapes at least 24 hours before serving.

damask cake

500–700 g/2½–3½ cups royal icing sugar/mix
red food colouring paste
2 quantities Basic Vanilla Cake (page 11)
1 quantity Meringue Buttercream (page 16)
300 g/10 oz. good jam, warmed and strained, or lemon curd
icing/confectioners' sugar, to dust
1 kg/36 oz. ready-to-roll royal icing
nonstick baking parchment
2 disposable piping bags
20-cm/8-inch and 15-cm/6-inch square cake pans, greased and baselined with greased baking parchment
20-cm/8-inch and 15-cm/6-inch square cake boards
dowel rods and shears

serves 20

Make the damask shapes at least 24 hours before you plan to serve the cakes. Trace your chosen shapes onto the baking parchment. Draw more than you will need, to allow for any accidents. Flip the paper over – you should be able to see the marks through the paper. (**1**)

Make the royal icing according to the pack instructions, gradually adding enough water until the icing is thick enough to hold a ribbon trail. Spoon 3 tablespoons of the icing into a bowl and tint dark pink using the food colouring paste. Tint the remaining icing a paler shade and cover with clingfilm/plastic wrap until ready to use. Spoon the darker icing into the piping bag and snip the end to a fine point. Carefully pipe a fine outline following the patterns you have traced. Let dry for 20 minutes. (**2**)

Add a drop more water to the other tinted icing to make it spreadable. Spoon into another piping bag and pipe inside the outlines so that it fills them in an even layer. Let dry for at least 24 hours. Cover any remaining icing. (**3**)

The next day, preheat the oven to 180°C (350°F) Gas 4. Prepare one quantity of the Basic Vanilla Cake mixture at a time as described on page 11. Divide evenly between the cake pans. Spread level and bake on the middle shelf of the preheated oven for 15–25 minutes depending

on the size of the cake. Let the cakes cool in the pans for 3–4 minutes, then turn out onto a wire rack to cool completely. Leave the oven on. Wash and dry the cake pans and prepare for baking as before. Prepare the second quantity of Vanilla Cake mixture, divide between the re-prepared pans and bake as above.

Place one of the larger cakes on the larger cake board and one smaller cake on a smaller board. Spread a layer of Meringue Buttercream, then a layer of jam over the tops. Cover with the matching layers, pressing them gently together. Cover the tops and sides of the cakes with a layer of buttercream and refrigerate for 30 minutes.

Dust the work surface with icing/confectioners' sugar and roll out two-thirds of the ready-to-roll royal icing until 2 mm/¹⁄₁₆ inch thick. Lay the icing over the large cake, smoothing the top and sides with your hands. Cut off any excess icing. Cover the smaller cake in the same way using the remaining icing. Let dry for 30 minutes.

Stack the cakes on top of one another using dowel rods as support (see page 100). Very carefully peel the damask shapes off the parchment and stick to the cake with a dab of royal icing. Pipe dots around the edges with any remaining royal icing. Let dry before serving.

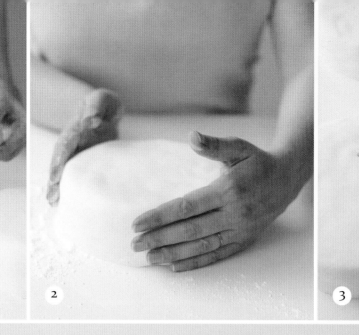

This three-tiered cake will make enough to feed about 60 people and is perfect for a christening or wedding. You should bake the cakes a week before you plan to serve them, to allow the flavours to mellow.

celebration cake

2 quantities Classic Rich Fruit Cake (page 13)

450 g/1 lb. apricot jam, warmed and strained

icing/confectioners' sugar, to dust

1 kg/36 oz. natural marzipan

2 kg/5 lbs. ready-to-roll royal icing

200 g/1 cup royal icing sugar

edible pearls, gold balls and sugar diamonds

25-cm/10-inch; 20-cm/8-inch; and 15-cm/6-inch round cake pans, greased and baselined with a double thickness of greased baking parchment

25-cm/10-inch; 20-cm/8-inch; and 15-cm/6-inch cake boards

dowel rods and shears

embossing tools (see page 18)

disposable piping bag

ribbon

serves about 60

Preheat the oven to 150°C (300°F) Gas 2.

Prepare the first quantity of Classic Rich Fruit Cake mixture as described on page 13, then spoon into the largest cake pan, scraping the mixture from the bowl using a rubber spatula. Spread level and bake in the bottom third of the preheated oven for about 2 hours. Cover the top of the cake with a sheet of baking parchment for the last hour to prevent it browning too quickly. A skewer inserted into the middle should come out clean. Let the cake cool in the pan on a wire rack and when completely cold, turn the cake out of the pan and wrap in clingfilm/plastic wrap until ready to assemble. Leave the oven on. Prepare the second quantity of Classic Rich Fruit Cake mixture and divide between the medium and small cake pans, filling each pan to the same depth. Bake in the bottom third of the oven for 1 hour 30 minutes, then let cool as above.

Place each cake on its matching cake board. Brush jam over the top and sides. Dust the work surface with icing/confectioners' sugar and roll out half the marzipan into a disc 45 cm/18 inches across. Roll the marzipan over the rolling pin and unroll over the large cake to cover. Smooth it over the cake and trim off any excess. Repeat with the medium cake and two-thirds of the remaining marzipan; and the small cake and the last of the marzipan. Lightly brush cooled, boiled water over the large cake. Dust a work surface with more sugar and roll out half the ready-to-roll icing into a disc about 50 cm/20 inches across. Carefully roll the icing over the rolling pin and unroll it over the cake, covering the top and sides. (1)

Gently smooth the icing and trim off any excess. Repeat with the medium cake and two-thirds of the remaining icing; and with the small cake and the last of the icing.(2).

Insert one piece of dowel rod into the large cake and make a note of the height of the cake. Remove the rod and, using shears, cut 4 pieces of dowel slightly longer than the height of the cake. Repeat with the medium cake. Insert 4 dowel rods in a square in the middle of the large and medium cakes. (3)

Use a palette knife to score criss-crossing lines across the tops of the cakes. Make patterns in the sides using embossing tools. Mix the royal icing sugar with a little cold water to form a thick paste, spoon into the piping bag and pipe dots around the top edge of the medium cake. Press pearls, gold balls and diamonds into the icing. Let the cakes dry completely. Stack them on top of one another using the dowel rods as support. Wrap ribbon around the bottom edge of each cake.

for the holidays

This rich, gluten-free chocolate cake is a delicious option for Easter. Under the glossy chocolate ganache is a lovely layer of marzipan to complement the ground almonds in the cake mixture. The chocolate shavings for the nest can be made in advance and kept in a container in the fridge until needed. Look for mini chocolate eggs in pretty coloured wrappers or covered in a speckled candy coating.

easter nest chocolate cake

1 tablespoon cocoa powder, plus extra to dust

300 g/10 oz. dark/bittersweet chocolate, chopped

200 g/14 tablespoons butter

6 large eggs, separated

200 g/1 cup (caster) sugar

50 g/¼ cup packed light brown soft sugar

2 teaspoons instant coffee granules dissolved in 2 teaspoons boiling water

175 g/1¾ cups ground almonds

¼ teaspoon cream of tartar

a pinch of salt

to decorate

5 tablespoons apricot jam

1 quantity Chocolate Ganache (page 14)

icing/confectioners' sugar, to dust

200 g/6½ oz. natural marzipan

dark/bittersweet, white and milk chocolate shavings (page 20)

mini chocolate eggs

two 20-cm/8-inch springform cake pans, greased and baselined with greased baking parchment

serves 10

Start making the cake the day before you want to serve it.

Preheat the oven to 170°C (325°F) Gas 3. Dust the cake pans with extra cocoa powder, tap on the work surface and tip out any excess.

Put the chocolate and butter in a heatproof bowl set over a pan of barely simmering water. Do not let the base of the bowl touch the water. Stir until smooth and thoroughly combined. Remove from the heat and cool slightly.

Put the egg yolks, 150 g/¾ cup of the (caster) sugar and all the light brown sugar in the bowl of a stand mixer and whisk until pale and very thick. Add the melted chocolate mixture and coffee and whisk to combine. Add the ground almonds, cocoa powder and stir to mix.

Whisk the egg whites, cream of tartar and salt in a clean bowl until they hold a soft peak. Add the remaining (caster) sugar and continue to whisk until the egg whites are stiff but not dry. Using a large metal spoon, stir a large spoonful of the egg whites into the chocolate mixture, then carefully fold in the remainder.

Divide the mixture evenly between the prepared pans and spread level with a palette knife. Bake the cakes on the middle shelf of the preheated oven for 35–40 minutes or until the cakes have risen, formed a light crust and a skewer inserted in the middle comes out with a moist crumb. Let cool in the pans for 3–4 minutes, then turn out onto a wire rack to cool completely. Wrap the cold cakes in clingfilm/plastic wrap and set aside until the following day.

The next day, gently heat the apricot jam to make it a little runnier, then strain it to get rid of any lumps.

Place one of the cake layers on a serving dish and spread a thin layer of the jam over it. Carefully spread 2 tablespoons of the Chocolate Ganache on top and cover with the second cake layer. Gently press the layers together. Lightly brush apricot jam over the whole cake.

Dust the work surface with icing/confectioners' sugar and roll out the marzipan into a disc about 35 cm/14 inches across. Roll the marzipan over the rolling pin and unroll over the cake to cover completely. Smooth it over the cake and trim off any excess. Brush a little more jam all over the marzipan and set aside for 5 minutes.

Using a palette knife, spread the remaining chocolate ganache smoothly over the top and side of the cake and let set in a cool place for about 30 minutes.

Arrange the chocolate shavings around the top of the cake in a nest shape and nestle the chocolate eggs in the middle.

I like to serve this cake for an autumnal celebration because of its warming spices, nuts, cream cheese and caramel filling. For the final flourish, the cake is enrobed in a layer of marshmallow frosting. I have kept the decoration minimal but you could scatter toasted nuts and maybe a sprinkling of ground cinnamon over the top, too. This cake would be ideal to serve at a family Thanksgiving get-together. All it needs with it is a roaring log fire and extra large cups of tea or hot chocolate.

spiced nut layer cake

100 g/⅔ cup shelled walnuts or pecans

300 g/2⅓ cups plain/all-purpose flour

2 teaspoons baking powder

1 teaspoon bicarbonate of/baking soda

1 teaspoon ground cinnamon

¼ teaspoon ground cloves

¼ teaspoon grated nutmeg

a pinch of salt

175 g/1½ sticks butter, soft

175 g/1 scant cup (caster) sugar

100 g/½ cup light muscovado or packed light brown soft sugar

3 large eggs, separated

1 teaspoon vanilla extract

250 ml/1 cup buttermilk, room temperature

½ quantity Cream Cheese Frosting (page 14)

200 g/6½ oz. dulce de leche

1 quantity Marshmallow Frosting (page 16)

three 20-cm/8-inch springform cake pans, greased and baselined with greased baking parchment

serves 10–12

Preheat the oven to 180°C (350°F) Gas 4.

Tip the walnuts onto a baking sheet and toast in the preheated oven for 4–5 minutes. Leave the oven on. Let the walnuts cool completely, then finely chop in a food processor.

Sift together the flour, baking powder, bicarbonate of/baking soda, spices and salt.

Cream the butter and both sugars in the bowl of a stand mixer until pale and light – at least 3–4 minutes. Gradually add the egg yolks to the creamed butter one at a time, mixing well between each addition and scraping down the bowl from time to time with a rubber spatula. Add the vanilla and ground walnuts and mix to incorporate.

Whisk the egg whites in a clean bowl until they hold a stiff peak.

Gradually add the sifted dry ingredients to the bowl alternately with the buttermilk and mix until smooth. Finally, fold in the egg whites using a large metal spoon. Divide the mixture evenly between the prepared cake pans, scraping the mixture from the bowl using a rubber spatula. Spread level and bake on the middle shelf of the preheated oven for about 25 minutes or until golden, well risen and a skewer inserted in the middle comes out clean. Let cool in the pans for 3–4 minutes, then turn out onto a wire rack to cool completely.

Place one of the cake layers on a serving dish and spread half the Cream Cheese Frosting over it. Top with half the dulce de leche and cover with a second cake layer. Repeat this process, finishing with the third cake layer. Press the cakes together gently.

Spread the Marshmallow Frosting evenly over the top and sides of the cake, creating peaks and generous swirls with a palette knife.

This is an unusual cake that sits somewhere between gingerbread and brownies. The spiced chocolate mixture is dense, dark and smokey, and would suit a Bonfire Night or Fourth of July celebration, or any other evening that features fireworks, sparklers and things that pop and sizzle. As the flavour improves after 24 hours, it's a good one to make ahead. Kugelhopf or bundt tins are now available in a variety of shapes and sizes from the very simple to the more elaborately shaped, like the one I've used here.

firecracker cake

175 g/1½ sticks butter, soft, plus extra to grease

cocoa powder, to dust

225 g/8 oz. dark/bittersweet chocolate, chopped

150 g/¾ cup packed light brown soft or light muscovado sugar

3 tablespoons maple or golden syrup

2 tablespoons dark treacle/molasses

2 nuggets of stem ginger in syrup, finely chopped, plus 3 tablespoons of the syrup

4 large eggs, lightly beaten

grated zest of 1 orange

125 g/1 cup plain/all-purpose flour

1½ teaspoons baking powder

1 teaspoon ground cinnamon

1 teaspoon ground ginger

½ teaspoon ground mixed spice/apple pie spice

½ teaspoon hot chilli powder

a pinch of salt

to decorate

175 g/6 oz. dark/bittersweet chocolate, finely chopped

125 ml/½ cup double/heavy cream

popping candy/space dust

chocolate sticks

orange and red sanding sugar

2-litre/quart capacity kugelhopf pan

serves 10

Preheat the oven to 170°C (325°F) Gas 3.

Melt a little of the extra butter and use to grease the cake pan, making sure that the pan is thoroughly and evenly coated. Dust the pan with cocoa powder and tip out any excess.

Put the chocolate, butter, sugar, syrup and treacle/molasses in a medium, heavy-based saucepan over low heat to melt – do not walk away from this pan and attempt to do the laundry, flower arranging or send some emails, but instead keep an eye on it and stir every 30 seconds until the mixture is glossy and silky smooth. Remove from the heat, pour into a large bowl and set aside to cool slightly.

Add the chopped stem ginger (reserving 3 tablespoons of the syrup), eggs and orange zest to the slightly cooled chocolate mixture and mix until thoroughly combined.

Sift together the flour, baking powder, spices and salt, then fold into the cake mixture until smooth.

Spoon the mixture into the prepared cake pan, spread level and bake just below the middle shelf of the preheated oven for about 45 minutes or until a skewer inserted into the middle comes out with a moist crumb.

Let cool in the pan for no more than 5 minutes, then carefully turn out onto a wire rack and let cool completely.

To decorate the cake, tip the chocolate into a heatproof bowl. Heat the cream and reserved stem ginger syrup in a small saucepan until boiling, then pour into the bowl of chocolate and let melt. Stir until smooth and let cool and thicken slightly.

Place the cake on a serving dish and carefully pour the molten chocolate cream over the cake so that it trickles down the sides. Let set slightly.

Scatter the popping candy/space dust and sanding sugar over the cake and top with chocolate sticks as logs and twigs.

This is an impressive yet surprisingly easy cake – ideal for Christmas or New Year's Eve. Most of the elements (the cake base, praline and chocolate cream frosting) can be made in advance and assembled on the day. I think it tastes even better the day after serving, so reserve a slice for a quiet moment.

hungarian dobos torte

plain/all-purpose flour, to dust
1 quantity Whisked Almond Cake (page 12)
1 quantity Rum or Brandy Syrup (page 17)
1 quantity Chocolate Cream Frosting (page 15)
½ quantity Chocolate Ganache (page 14)

almond praline
125 g/⅔ cup (caster) sugar
100 g/⅔ cup blanched almonds

three 20-cm/8-inch springform cake pans, greased and baselined with greased baking parchment

baking sheet, oiled

serves 8–10

Start making the cake the day before you want to serve it.

Preheat the oven to 180°C (350°F) Gas 4. Dust the cake pans with a little flour and tip out any excess.

Prepare the Whisked Almond Cake mixture as described on page 12, then divide evenly between the prepared pans and spread level with a palette knife. Bake the cakes on the middle shelf of the preheated oven for about 15–20 minutes or until golden, well risen and a skewer inserted into the middle comes out clean. Let cool in the pans for 3–4 minutes, then turn out onto a wire rack to cool completely.

Wrap the cold cakes in clingfilm/plastic wrap and set aside until the following day.

To make the almond praline, put the sugar and 3 tablespoons water in a small, heavy-based saucepan over low heat. Cook to completely dissolve the sugar. Bring to the boil and cook, swirling the pan occasionally, until the syrup turns to an amber-coloured caramel. Tip the almonds into the pan and cook for 1 minute. Now tip everything out onto the oiled baking sheet. Set aside to cool completely.

When the block of caramel almonds is completely cold and hardened, break off one third, roughly chop, and set aside to decorate the cake later. Snap the remainder into pieces and whizz in a food processor until it is the texture of coarse sand.

When you are ready to assemble the cake, using a long serrated knife, slice each of the cakes in half horizontally to make 6 layers of even thickness. (**1**)

Place one of the cake layers on a serving dish and brush some of the Rum or Brandy Syrup over it. Spread 2 tablespoons of Chocolate Cream Frosting smoothly over that using a palette knife and top with 1 tablespoon of the ground praline. Cover with another cake layer. Repeat this process until you have used up all the cake layers and praline. (**2**)

Spread the remaining frosting over top and sides of the cake and refrigerate for 10 minutes. (**3**)

Spread the Chocolate Ganache on top of the cake and allow it to drip over the sides. Set aside in a cool place until ready to serve. Just before serving, scatter the reserved caramelized almonds on top of the cake .

A pile of sparkling, sugar-crusted fruit sits on top of a delicate flutter of silver leaf, making this simple, festive fruit cake something really rather special. You can use any number of fruits to top this cake – why not try frosting small apples and pears? Edible silver leaf is available at sugarcraft stores or online but if you prefer you could always lightly dust the finished cake with edible glitter.

frosted christmas fruit cake

1 quantity Classic Rich Fruit Cake (page 13)

4 tablespoons apricot jam

icing/confectioners' sugar, to dust

250 g/8 oz. natural marzipan

250 g/8 oz. ready-to-roll royal icing

edible silver leaf

frosted fruit

fresh cherries

red and white grapes

physalis/cape gooseberries

strands of redcurrants

1 large egg white, very lightly whisked

300 g/1½ cups caster/ superfine sugar

deep 20-cm/8-inch round cake pan, greased and lined with a double thickness of greased baking parchment

baking parchment

kitchen twine

festive ribbon

serves 8–10

Preheat the oven to 150°C (300°F) Gas 2. Wrap the outside of the cake pan in a double thickness of baking parchment and secure with kitchen twine.

Prepare the Classic Rich Fruit Cake mixture as described on page 13, then spoon into the cake pan, scraping the mixture from the bowl using a rubber spatula. Spread level and bake in the bottom third of the preheated oven for about 2 hours. Cover the top of the cake with a sheet of baking parchment for the last hour to prevent it browning too quickly. A skewer inserted into the middle should come out clean. Let the cake cool in the pan on a wire rack and when completely cold, turn the cake out of the pan and wrap in clingfilm/plastic wrap until ready to assemble.

To make the frosted fruit, take one piece of fruit at a time and lightly brush egg white all over it with a soft pastry brush. Coat evenly in caster/superfine sugar, then let dry on baking parchment or on a wire rack for at least 2 hours until it looks frosty. Repeat with all the remaining fruit.

When you are ready to assemble the cake, gently heat the apricot jam to make it a little runnier, then strain it to get rid of any lumps.

Place the cake on a serving dish and brush a thin layer of jam on top of it.

Dust the work surface with icing/confectioners' sugar and roll out the marzipan into a disc slightly larger than the top of the cake. Using the cake pan as a guide, cut out a neat circle and lay this on top of the cake. Brush a little more jam over the marzipan and set aside for 5 minutes.

Roll and cut out the ready-to-roll royal icing as above. Place this disc directly on top of the marzipan. Crimp the edge of the icing, all the way around, by gently pinching the icing between your thumb and forefinger at regular intervals along the edge. Let dry for about 1 hour.

Lightly brush boiling water on top of the icing. Using a fine, clean craft brush, apply the silver leaf to the icing so that it flutters and creates a craggy surface on the cake. Arrange the frosted fruits on top. Tie festive ribbon around the cake.

To cut out the star shapes for this cake you will need to make templates from paper or baking parchment. The spiced brown sugar pound cake is full of the evocative, warming spices of Christmas and any leftover bits would be delicious in a festive trifle, ensuring that you don't waste a single delicious crumb.

stack of glittery stars

spiced brown sugar pound cake – you will need to make TWICE this quantity

225 g/2 sticks butter, soft

200 g/1 cup light muscovado sugar

100 g/½ cup (caster) sugar

4 large eggs, lightly beaten

350 g/1⅔ cups plain/all-purpose flour

2½ teaspoons baking powder

1 teaspoon ground cinnamon

1 teaspoon ground ginger

½ teaspoon ground mixed spice/ apple pie spice

a pinch of salt

175 ml/⅔ cup buttermilk, room temperature

to decorate

1 quantity Meringue Buttercream (page 16, but follow the method on this page)

1 teaspoon ground cinnamon

assorted gold and silver edible balls

30 x 40 x 4-cm baking pan, greased and lined with greased baking parchment

4 star-shaped paper templates in different sizes, eg 23 cm/9 inches, 20 cm/8 inches, 15 cm/6 inches and 10 cm/4 inches plus 2 small sizes of template or 2 small sizes of star-shaped cookie cutters

serves 8–10

Start making the cake the day before you want to serve it.

Preheat the oven to 180°C (350°F) Gas 4.

To make the first batch of spiced brown sugar pound cake, cream the butter and sugar in the bowl of a stand mixer until really pale and light – at least 3–4 minutes. Gradually add the beaten eggs in 4 or 5 additions, mixing well between each addition and scraping down the bowl from time to time with a rubber spatula.

Sift the flour, baking powder, spices and salt into the bowl, add the buttermilk and mix again until silky smooth and thoroughly combined. Transfer the mixture to the prepared baking pan and spread level using a palette knife. Bake on the middle shelf of the preheated oven for about 25 minutes until golden brown, well risen and a skewer inserted into the middle comes out clean.

Let cool in the pan for 10 minutes, then turn out onto a wire rack to cool completely.

Make a second batch of spiced brown sugar pound cake, following the method above.

When both cakes are cold, wrap in clingfilm/plastic wrap and refrigerate until the following day.

When you are ready to assemble the cake, make the Meringue Buttercream as described on page 16, but replace the vanilla with the cinnamon and fold in gently.

Work out how best to make all the templates fit on the cake layers before you start cutting! You are probably best to lay the 23–cm/9-inch, 15-cm/6-inch and one or 2 of the smallest stars on one cake layer, and the other templates on the second cake layer. Cut carefully around the templates using a sharp knife. Spread some of the cinnamon meringue buttercream over each star cake.

Place the largest star cake on a serving dish and stack the remaining stars on top in decreasing sizes. Scatter gold and silver edible balls over the visible buttercream.

meringue mushrooms

1 quantity Super-duper Disco Meringues (see page 57, but follow the method on this page)

1½ tablespoons cocoa powder, plus extra to dust

75 g/2½ oz. dark/bittersweet chocolate, chopped

bûche de noël

225 g/8 oz. dark/bittersweet chocolate, chopped

50 g/½ cup plain/all-purpose flour

2 tablespoons cocoa powder

a pinch of salt

8 large eggs, separated

225 g/1¼ cups (caster) sugar

a pinch of cream of tartar

1 teaspoon vanilla extract

75 g/5 tablespoons butter, melted

1 quantity Mocha Meringue Buttercream (page 17)

icing/confectioners' sugar, to dust

2 large piping bags, fitted with plain 1-cm/⅜-inch nozzles/tips

baking sheets, lined with baking parchment

35 x 25-cm/14 x 10-in. Swiss-roll/jelly-roll pan and 26 x 17-cm/10½ x 7-in. baking pan, greased and lined with large sheets of greased baking parchment

ornamental robins

serves 6–8

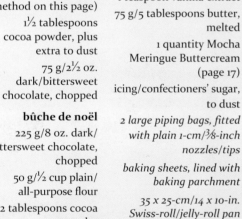

The adorable meringue mushrooms are what make this cake so special, so have a go at making them – they're easier than you might think!

bûche de noël

Make the meringue mushrooms 24 hours in advance. Preheat the oven to 110°C (225°F) Gas ¼. Prepare the Super-duper Meringue mixture as described on page 57 and divide between 2 bowls. Beat the cocoa powder into one bowl. Spoon each mixture into separate piping bags. Pipe about 25–30 brown domes onto the prepared baking sheets. These will be the mushroom caps. Flatten the peaks with a wet fingertip. Pipe about 25–30 white cones in assorted sizes for the stalks. (**1**)

Bake in the preheated oven for 1 hour. Remove from the oven and let cool before serving. Turn the oven up to 170°C (325°F) Gas 3.

Melt the chocolate in a heatproof bowl set over pans of barely simmering water, stirring until smooth. Do not let the base of the bowl touch the water. Make a 2-mm/¹⁄₁₆-inch hole in the base of each mushroom cap with a wooden skewer. Spread a thin layer of melted chocolate over the base and let set. (**2**)

Stand the stalks upright and very carefully push the points into the holes in the mushroom caps. Let dry. (**3**)

To make the bûche de noël, melt the chocolate as described above. Sift together the flour, cocoa powder and the salt. Tip the egg yolks and 150 g/¾ cup of the (caster) sugar into the bowl of a stand mixer and whisk until thick and pale. Put the egg whites and cream of tartar in a large, clean bowl and whisk until they will hold a soft peak. Add the remaining sugar and whisk until stiff but not dry.

Fold the melted chocolate and vanilla into the egg-yolk mixture. Add the sifted ingredients and mix well. Add one-third of the beaten egg whites and fold in, then add the remaining egg whites, carefully folding in. Fold in the melted butter.

Spoon two-thirds of the mixture into the larger prepared pan and the remaining mixture into the smaller one. Spread level. Bake on the middle shelf of the preheated oven for 10–12 minutes, swapping the pans around halfway through baking. Let cool for 2 minutes, then slide the cakes, still on the parchment, onto wire racks. Cover loosely with tea towels. Let cool completely.

Lay a sheet of baking parchment on top of the large cake and place a baking sheet on top of that. Holding the wire rack and the baking sheet, quickly flip the cake over. Peel off the baking paper and spread 8 tablespoons of the Mocha Meringue Buttercream over the cake. Using the clean paper to help you, roll the cake up from a shorter end into a tight roll. Repeat this process with the small cake and 5 tablespoons of the buttercream.

Arrange the larger roll on a serving dish. Cut the smaller roll in half on the diagonal and place the pieces on either side of the larger roll at an angle. Cover with buttercream and use a knife to create a bark effect. Top with meringue mushrooms, robins and a dusting of icing/confectioners' sugar and cocoa powder.

This fruit and ginger-packed cake is a great, lighter alternative to a traditional Christmas cake but can be served for any festive occasion. It looks fabulous when decorated with a selection of beautiful whole glacé fruits, which are available from specialist grocers and food halls. If you prefer, you can simply cover the top of the cake in a selection of nuts and a light glaze of apricot jam. Ginger wine is more usually to be found in a Whisky Mac cocktail but it works a treat in this cake. If you can't find it, you could substitute Marsala or brandy.

date & ginger cake

200 g/6½ oz. ready-to-eat pitted dates

4 nuggets of stem ginger in syrup, plus 3 tablespoons of the syrup

175 g/1¼ cups sultanas/golden raisins

175 g/1¼ cups raisins

grated zest and juice of 1 lemon

grated zest and juice of 1 orange

5 tablespoons ginger wine

200 g/1¾ cups plain/all-purpose flour

2 teaspoons baking powder

1 tablespoon ground ginger

2 teaspoons ground mixed spice/apple pie spice

50 g/⅓ cup ground almonds

200 g/13 tablespoons butter, soft

100 g/½ cup light muscovado sugar

100 g/½ cup dark muscovado sugar

3 large eggs, lightly beaten

2 tablespoons milk

lemon & ginger syrup

2 tablespoons demerara sugar

juice of ½ lemon

juice of ½ orange

3 tablespoons ginger wine

to decorate

2 tablespoons apricot jam

assorted glacé fruits, eg pears, clementines, kumquats, cherries

assorted shelled nuts eg pistachios, almonds, brazil nuts

23-cm/9-inch round cake pan

ribbon

serves 10

Prepare the dried fruit a good couple of hours before you plan to bake the cake. Chop the dates into pieces roughly the same size as the raisins and finely chop the stem ginger (reserving 3 tablespoons of the syrup). Mix the dates, ginger, sultanas/golden raisins, raisins and lemon and orange zests and juices in a large saucepan. Add the ginger wine, stir well and cook over low heat for a couple of minutes until the liquid is hot but not boiling. Stir the fruit well, remove from the heat and set aside until the fruit has plumped up and absorbed almost all the liquid. Stir occasionally. Let cool completely before using in the cake mixture.

When you are ready to bake the cake, preheat the oven to 150°C (300°F) Gas 2. Grease the cake pan and line it with a double thickness of greased baking parchment.

Sift together the flour, baking powder, spices and ground almonds.

Cream the butter and sugars in the bowl of a stand mixer until pale and light – at least 3–4 minutes. Gradually add the beaten eggs to the creamed butter in 4 or 5 additions, mixing well between each addition and scraping down the bowl from time to time with a rubber spatula.

Using a large metal spoon, fold the sifted dry ingredients and plumped fruits (and any remaining liquid) into the mixture and stir until thoroughly combined. Add the milk and mix again, then divide the mixture evenly between the prepared cake pan, scraping the mixture from the bowl using a rubber spatula. Spread level and bake on the middle shelf of the preheated oven for about 1 hour 30–45 minutes. Loosely cover the top of the cake with a sheet of baking parchment halfway though baking if it appears to be browning too quickly. The cake is cooked when a skewer inserted into the middle comes out with a moist crumb.

While the cake is baking, make the lemon & ginger syrup. Put all ingredients and the reserved stem ginger syrup into a small saucepan over medium heat. Bring to the boil and stir to dissolve the sugar. Simmer for about 5 minutes or until reduced by one-third. Remove from the heat and let cool.

Remove the baked cake from the oven and let cool in the pan for 10 minutes. Prick the cake all over with a wooden skewer and pour the lemon & ginger syrup slowly over the top, allowing it to soak in. Let cool completely in the cake pan.

Once the cake is completely cold, remove from the pan and wrap in baking parchment or foil and foil until ready to decorate.

To decorate, melt the apricot jam in a small saucepan with 1 tablespoon water. Strain the jam to get rid of any lumps and brush an even layer over the top of the cake. Arrange the glacé fruits and nuts over the top and tie a ribbon around the outside.

This is a very simple way of giving a splash of colour to your festive cake. I have chosen to use a frosty blue for my icing but you really could use any colour you like – red and green would also work very well for a Christmas-themed cake, as would simple snowflake shapes for the cut-outs. Why not emboss patterns into the cut-out shapes (see page 18) and then use them to decorate the cake too?

blue & white starry cake

1 quantity Classic Rich Fruit Cake (page 13)

4 tablespoons apricot jam

icing/confectioners' sugar, to dust

500 g/1 lb. natural marzipan

700 g/24 oz. ready-to-roll fondant icing

blue food colouring paste

edible blue metallic balls

edible silver balls

white sugar balls

deep 23-cm/9-inch round cake pan, greased and lined with a double thickness of greased baking parchment

baking parchment

kitchen twine

star-shaped cookie cutters

festive ribbon

serves 8–10

Preheat the oven to 150°C (300°F) Gas 2. Wrap the outside of the cake pan in a double thickness of baking parchment and secure with kitchen twine.

Prepare the Classic Rich Fruit Cake mixture as described on page 13, then spoon into the cake pan, scraping the mixture from the bowl using a rubber spatula. Spread level and bake in the bottom third of the preheated oven for about 2 hours. Cover the top of the cake with a sheet of baking parchment for the last hour to prevent it browning too quickly. A skewer inserted into the middle should come out clean. Let the cake cool in the pan on a wire rack and when completely cold, turn the cake out of the pan and wrap in clingfilm/plastic wrap until ready to assemble.

When you are ready to assemble the cake, gently heat the apricot jam to make it a little runnier, then strain it to get rid of any lumps.

Place the cake on a serving dish and brush a thin layer of jam over the top and sides.

Dust the work surface with icing/confectioners' sugar and roll out the marzipan into a disc 40 cm/16 inches across. Roll the marzipan over the rolling pin and unroll over the cake to cover completely. Smooth it over the cake and trim off any excess.

Using the food colouring paste, tint half the fondant icing a pale shade of blue. Roll out as described above. Very lightly brush cool boiled water over the marzipan.

Roll the icing over the rolling pin and unroll over the cake to cover the marzipan completely. Smooth it over the cake and trim off any excess.

Roll the remaining white icing out as described above. Lightly brush cool boiled water over the top edge and the bottom of the sides of the icing. Roll the icing over the rolling pin and unroll over the cake to cover completely. Smooth it over the cake and trim off any excess. Crimp the icing, all the way around the top edge, by gently pinching the icing between your thumb and forefinger at regular intervals.

Using the cookie cutters, stamp out stars from the sides and top of the cake, pushing the cutters just through the white icing. Carefully remove the cutters and the white star, leaving the blue icing exposed.

Push edible blue balls into the crimped edge of the cake and fill some of the star shapes with silver and more blue balls. Gently push white and blue balls into or above some of the tips of the stars. Finally, tie a ribbon around the base of the cake.

I love making use of decoratively shaped cake pans, especially at Christmas or the holidays. Individual kugelhopf pans are probably my favourite, and are available online or in good kitchenware stores. These clementine cakes add a certain wow to the tea table with their flurry of gold leaf and candied peel. You could even package them in festive boxes and ribbons – surely everyone loves to receive a cake as a gift?

clementine & pistachio cakes

3 tablespoons icing/
confectioners' sugar

edible gold leaf

candied clementine peel

2 clementines

100 g/½ cup (caster) sugar,
plus extra to sprinkle

clementine & pistachio cake

1 tablespoon melted butter to
grease the cake pans

2 clementines

100 g/⅔ cup shelled, unsalted
pistachios

75 g/¾ cup ground almonds

100 g/¾ cup plain/all-purpose
flour, plus extra to dust

1½ teaspoons baking powder

½ teaspoon ground cinnamon

a pinch of salt

3 large eggs

150 g/¾ cup (caster) sugar

spiced citrus syrup

juice of 1 lemon

100 g/½ cup (caster) sugar

1 cinnamon stick

4 cardamom pods, bruised

2 star anise

six 10-cm/4-inch kugelhopf pans

makes 6

You will need to make the candied clementine peel the day before you want to make the cakes. Wash the clementines. Squeeze the juice, cover and set aside. Using a teaspoon, carefully scrape out any tough membrane from the inside of the squeezed out clementine shells. Cut the peel into slices about 5 mm/½ inch thick. Bring a small saucepan of water to the boil, add the peel and simmer for 2 minutes. Drain and repeat this process, boiling with fresh water, a further 2 times.

Put the sugar into the cleaned-out pan, add 100 ml/½ cup water and bring slowly to the boil to dissolve the sugar. Add the clementine peel and simmer gently for about 30–40 minutes until tender and translucent. Using a slotted spoon remove the peel from the syrup and arrange in a single layer on a wire rack. Let dry overnight.

The next day, toss the dried peel in a little extra (caster) sugar and store in an airtight container.

When you are ready to bake the cakes, refrigerate the kugelhopf pans for 10 minutes. Carefully, and very thoroughly, brush the insides with melted butter. Dust with flour and tap out any excess.

Wash the clementines, place in a small saucepan, cover with cold water and bring to the boil. Simmer gently for about 45 minutes or until really tender. Drain and let cool.

Preheat the oven to 180°C (350°F) Gas 4.

Whizz the pistachios in a food processor until finely ground. Add the almonds, flour, baking powder, cinnamon and salt and whizz for a further 10 seconds. Tip into a bowl. Cut the cooked clementines in half and scoop out any pips. Roughly chop the fruit – skin and all – tip into the food processor and whizz until almost smooth.

Put the eggs and sugar in the bowl of a stand mixer and whisk on high speed until very thick, pale and the mixture will leave a ribbon trail when the whisk is lifted from the bowl. Fold in the clementine purée using a large metal spoon, followed by the sifted dry ingredients. Divide the batter between the prepared kugelhopf pans and place them on a baking sheet. Bake on the middle shelf of the preheated oven for about 30 minutes or until well risen, golden brown and a skewer inserted into the middle of the cakes comes out clean.

While the cakes are baking, make the spiced citrus syrup. Pour half the reserved clementine juice into a small pan, add the remaining ingredients and bring slowly to the boil to dissolve the sugar. Simmer for 2–3 minutes or until reduced by one-third. Remove from the heat and let cool.

Remove the cakes from the oven and let cool in the pans for 2 minutes. Turn the cakes out onto a wire rack, brush the syrup over them and let cool completely.

Whisk together the remaining clementine juice and just enough of the icing/confectioners' sugar to make a runny icing. Spoon over each cake. Let set for 5 minutes, then decorate with a flourish of gold leaf and some candied peel.

I love this cake for its quiet sophistication. It's also perfect for getting the kids involved because they can help to make the holly. Holly leaf-shaped cutters are often available in packs of assorted sizes and the leaves can be made days before you want to serve the cake. Store in airtight boxes until ready to use.

holly wreath fruit cake

1 quantity Classic Rich Fruit Cake (page 13)

200 g/6½ oz. gum or sugar florist paste

green food colouring paste

icing/confectioners' sugar, to dust

4 tablespoons apricot jam

500 g/1 lb. natural marzipan

500 g/1 lb. ready-to-roll royal icing

red food colouring paste

green edible glitter

deep 20-cm/8-inch. round cake pan, greased and lined with a double thickness of greased baking parchment

kitchen twine

assorted holly leaf-shaped cookie cutters

festive ribbon

serves 8–10

Preheat the oven to 150°C (300°F) Gas 2. Wrap the outside of the cake pan in a double thickness of baking parchment and secure with kitchen twine.

Prepare the Classic Rich Fruit Cake mixture as described on page 13, then spoon into the cake pan, scraping the mixture from the bowl using a rubber spatula. Spread level and bake in the bottom third of the preheated oven for about 2 hours. Cover the top of the cake with a sheet of baking parchment for the last hour to prevent it browning too quickly. A skewer inserted into the middle should come out clean. Let the cake cool in the pan on a wire rack and when completely cold, turn the cake out of the pan and wrap in clingfilm/plastic wrap until ready to assemble.

To make holly leaves, tint the gum paste green using the food colouring paste. Break off a nugget of gum paste and keep the rest tightly wrapped in clingfilm/plastic wrap to prevent it from drying out. Very lightly dust the work surface with icing/confectioners' sugar and roll the paste out to a thickness of 1–2 mm/¹⁄₁₆ inch. Using the holly leaf-shaped cutters, stamp out as many leaves as possible from the paste. Score fine lines with the tip of a knife to make veins and press and pinch the ends of the leaves into curly points. Arrange on a large piece of scrunched up baking parchment – this will help the leaves to crinkle and curl even more. Repeat with the remaining green paste. Let dry for at least 8 hours.

When you are ready to assemble the cake, gently heat the apricot jam to make it a little runnier, then strain it to get rid of any lumps. Place the cake on a serving dish and brush a thin layer of jam over the top and sides.

Dust the work surface with icing/confectioners' sugar and roll out the marzipan into a disc 35 cm/14 inches across. Roll the marzipan over the rolling pin and unroll over the cake to cover completely. Smooth it over the cake and trim off any excess. Lightly brush cooled, boiled water over the large cake. Dust a work surface with more sugar and roll out the ready-to-roll royal icing as described above. Carefully roll the icing over the rolling pin and unroll it over the cake, covering the top and sides. Gently smooth the icing and trim off any excess.

Use any white icing off-cuts to make the holly berries. Tint the icing red using the food colouring paste and roll into tiny balls.

Using a small craft brush, very lightly brush cold water over the tops of the holly leaves and sprinkle green edible glitter on them. Dab the underside of each leaf with water and arrange as a wreath on top of the covered cake. Position the berries among the leaves and finish by tying a ribbon around the cake.

index

acknowledgments

Creating this book would not have been possible without a mega-star team of super talented girls – all of whom I've had the joy of working with on many other projects.

Rachel, without whose incredible help I would be a jibbering wreck on a super-sugar-high. Not only does she bake a mean cake but she ensures that everyone is fed, watered and happy at all times.

Lady Céline, I feel enormously lucky that Céline was given the task of editing my first book nearly 4 years ago and has since been my eyes, brains and über-ed for another 8 books – it's hard to believe! Her patience, wisdom and good humour know no bounds.

Iona, whose vision in putting the words and pictures together has yet again been nothing short of brilliant and her creative skills even go as far as making the most gorgeous bunting ever. Thank you too for finding happy homes for mountains of cakes at the end of each day's photography.

Kate, who is never fazed by me filling her studio and kitchen full of all things sweet, has again created a book full of beautiful photographs.

Liz, who is the provider of a seemingly endless supply of fabulous tableware, and cake stands in every shape, size and colour imaginable.

And the boys:

Hughie, for tasting almost all the cakes in this book without complaint!

And Mungo, who'll never be able to read or bake a cake but has an instinctive knack for letting me know when it's time to put down the wooden spoon and mixing bowl and go for a long walk over the hills.

stockists & suppliers

UK

Cakes Cookies & Crafts Shop

www.cakescookiesandcraftsshop.co.uk

Tel: 01524 389 684

Bakeware and cake decorations, plus an extensive range of Wilton piping bag nozzles in all sorts of shapes and sizes. Also, lustres, sugar strands, nonpareils, sprinkles, glitter and sugar flowers, including the yellow wafer flowers from page 74.

Jane Asher

www.jane-asher.co.uk

Tel: 020 7584 6177

Shop and online supplier of a wide range of cake baking and decorating supplies, for example tiny assorted cutters and embossing tools.

John Lewis

www.johnlewis.com

Tel: 08456 049 049

Lovely range of bakeware, from vintage-style mixing bowls and measuring cups to seasonal and shaped cupcake cases and pretty cookie cutters.

Lakeland

www.lakeland.co.uk

Tel: 01539 488 100

See online for details of your nearest store. Huge selection of kitchen and baking equipment, such as cupcake pans, cake decorations, storage containers, etc. Plus a selection of flower-shaped cutters in a range of sizes.

Squires Kitchen

www.squires-shop.com

Tel: 0845 22 55 671

Large retailer of cake decorating and sugarcraft supplies with more than 4,000 products, for example, edible gold and silver leaf.

US

Crate & Barrel

www.crateandbarrel.com

Tel: 800 967 6696

Store and online supplier of kitchenware, such as muffin pans, silicone bakeware, seasonal paper cases and sugar thermometers.

Kitchen Krafts

www.kitchenkrafts.com

Tel: 800 298 5389

Lots and lots of bakeware, candy, cake decorating tools and ready-made icings, cookie cutters and piping bags and nozzles/tips.

Sugarcraft

www.sugarcraft.com

Every type of cake decoration imaginable, plus boxes for presenting and carrying cupcakes, cakes, and cookies as gifts.

Sur la Table

www.surlatable.com

Tel: 800 243 0852

Check online for details of your nearest store. Offers bakeware including kugelhopf/bundt pans. Good source for specialty ingredients too, such as ready-to-roll royal icing. More than 70 retail stores nationwide and an extensive online site.

Williams-Sonoma

www.williams-sonoma.com

Tel: 1 877 812 6235

Cupcake and muffin pans, cake stands, and more.

Wilton

www.wilton.com

The site to browse for all manner of baking and decorating supplies. Packed with patterned and themed paper cases, sprinkles, food colouring, and decorations to suit every possible occasion and theme.